COREY
CALLIGANO

I'm Still Here

Visit our website at www.StillwaterPress.com for more information.

First Stillwater River Publications Edition

ISBN-13: 978-1-94-6300-43-0
ISBN-10: 1-946-300-43-8

1 2 3 4 5 6 7 8 9 10
Written by Corey Calligano
Cover Design by Mikahla Dawson
Published by Stillwater River Publications, Glocester, RI, USA

Publisher's Cataloging-In-Publication Data
(Prepared by The Donohue Group, Inc.)

Names: Calligano, Corey.
Title: I'm still here : journaling through the pink ribbon / by Corey Calligano.
Description: First Stillwater River Publications edition. | Glocester, RI, USA : Stillwater River, [2017]
Identifiers: ISBN 9781946300430 | ISBN 1946300438
Subjects: LCSH: Calligano, Corey--Diaries. | Breast--Cancer--Patients--Biography. | Breast--Cancer--Patients--Diaries. | Breast--Cancer--Psychological aspects. | Breast--Cancer--Treatment. | LCGFT: Autobiographies.
Classification: LCC RC280.B8 C35 2017 | DDC 362.196994490092--dc23

Dedication

Olivia, Alaina and Landon, I wouldn't have fought so hard and wanted to live so much if I didn't have your three little faces to wake up to every morning.

Thank you for saving my life.

Mommy loves you.

Chapter 1

WTF

"Ummmm... What the hell is this?" That's what I said to myself in the shower, the night I found a lump in my breast. Actually, I probably said WTF but it's only the first line of my book and I didn't want to scare you off too quickly.

"It can't be, Corey calm down, I'm sure it's nothing." That's what I kept saying to myself as I was washing up in the shower. I needed a second opinion, so I got out of the shower, threw my bathrobe on and stormed out the bathroom and into my bedroom where my boyfriend was sitting on the bed. I pretty much asked him to feel up my left breast, to see if he could feel the lump that I was feeling and what guy is gonna turn down an opportunity to go to second base anyway? He felt around, told me he was concerned and that I should get it checked out. The very next day I called my primary doctor and got an appointment to come in that same day, to check out "WTF" this lump was. I don't mess around, especially when it comes to my health, this wasn't something I was going to brush off.

Sitting on the table in the doctor's office, I was thinking to myself, this is probably nothing, probably just a cyst. The doctor came in and I told her my concern, so she felt around my breast and immediately said "Oh, ok, ummm you can get dressed and I will be back in to tell you what action we are going to take. " What action we are going to take? So maybe not a cyst? When the doctor came back in she said she did in fact feel something round and hard and that I should get a mammogram and possibly an ultrasound. Three days later I had my very first mammogram, which if you've never had one isn't really that bad. It's uncomfortable, mostly squishing and pulling boobs left and right, but hands down the easiest test I've had thus far. After the mammogram was done, they did in fact, need to perform an ultrasound because the radiologist didn't see very much on the mammogram that could tell them what exactly was going on... Aye! This is totally my luck!

Ultrasound, another easy but uncomfortable test. Anyone that has ever had a baby, knows what an ultrasound is. Thankfully I didn't have to drink a bunch of water until my bladder was ready to explode, all the mommys out there know what I'm talking about. No, no, no this ultrasound was done right on my boob, right where the lump was. The ultrasound came back that yes, I did have something there and we needed more testing to see if in fact it could be cancerous. And the dreaded word was said....

BIOPSY... oh how I hate that word. If you're having a biopsy, your doctors are thinking you could have cancer. The biopsy I had was ultrasound guided. So, a tech held the ultrasound wand on my breast, on the "WTF" spot and a specialist numbed the area and "punched" out some tissue from the lump that I found. I say "punched" because I relate it to a hole puncher, like you use on paper. This hurt. After it was over I went home and stuck frozen veggies on my left boob for the entire night.

I have to tell you, the biopsy hurt, but what hurt the most was the waiting... thinking about what was happening and not being able to do anything about it. I cried a lot within those couple days. I received a call from my primary doctor the day after my biopsy, asking me to come in the next morning and to bring my mother. Bring my mother??! I knew right then, this was not going to be good news... which made the water works flow yet again.

My mom and I went into the doctor's office that next morning, my doctor walked in said hello, how are you and tried to make small talk. I looked at my doctor and said "Ok, give me the bad news." She said "Yes, it's breast cancer." BREAST CANCER....

Chapter 2

September 25, 2012

Horrible Words

I was in utter shock leaving the doctor's office after I received the bad news that I did, in fact, have breast cancer. I was crying, my mom was crying, and the only thought that was racing through my mind was, *I'm going to die*. We left the doctor's office and got in my car. My mom called my sister to tell her the shitty news. I called my boyfriend and when he answered, I didn't think I could actually get the words out. "I... umm... I have breast cancer." That's all I could say and I immediately started crying again. That was the first time I had said those horrible words out loud.

I was able to get an appointment with a breast surgeon five days after I walked out of my doctor's office,. Remember how I said waiting hurt the most? I now had five days of waiting, five days of thinking to myself that I was going to die in my thirties and leave three little children behind, never really knowing who their mother was. This is how I was thinking for five days. (I will get to my kids soon, keep reading.)

No one could console me. My friends and family all tried to comfort me, but I wasn't hearing it. I would say, "I know, I will be okay" or "I know,

I'm not dying" or "yes, I'm fine!!!" That's what I told everyone, but was I fine? NOPE! I cried around the clock, and explaining why I was crying to my eight-year-old and six-year-old daughters wasn't easy. I made up a lot of stories so my little girls wouldn't think anything was wrong with their mommy.

"Mommy, are you crying?"

"No, my allergies are awful today."

"Mommy, are you crying?"

"No, silly. My contacts are just bothering me."

"Mommy, it looks like you're crying."

"I'm fine, I'm not crying. I just poked myself in the eye!" I was running out of things to say. I knew I had to tell them what was really going on but I wanted to see that surgeon first.

My mom and my boyfriend went with me to my appointment to meet my soon-to-be breast surgeon. We waited in the waiting room, which for me seemed like forever! Finally, three women in lab coats came out and called my name. To me, one doctor coming out to get you from the waiting room is a bit off, they usually have their assistant come get you, but three doctors?! I was freaking out. The surgeon, the two physician assistants (PA from now on), my mom, my boyfriend, and I all piled into this tiny office. The surgeon explained to us that I have two tumors in my left breast that are growing aggressively. So, we can't just wait until I get my head on straight and process this, we need to take action soon. The cancer that I have is 90% estrogen-driven. Awesome. So in other words, being a female is killing me. The surgeon also explained that I am positive for a protein that promotes the growth of cancer cells called HER2. (I know, that was a lot of info... and breath.) HER2 goes along with breast cancer, but some people get lucky and don't get it. I'm not so lucky, I got it. Because (and I hope my fifth-grade teacher isn't reading this, she always said "Do not start a sentence with the word 'because'" - sorry, but I'm doing it.) I tested positive for Estrogen and HER2, this is actually a good thing, my chances for survival are greater. The surgeon also told us that I will have to have surgery, chemotherapy, and radiation. My first question was, "What stage am I at?" I don't know why I asked that, I've seen it on TV shows and in movies, and they seem to always know what stage they are, so I thought it was important to ask. The surgeon explained that she couldn't tell us that information yet because I needed some more testing. Great! More frigging tests! She explained that just from the mammogram and ultrasound she wasn't able to see a three-dimensional picture of the tumors to tell how big they actually are. I needed to have an MRI. Ugh, I'm very claustrophobic! First though, the surgeon explained that I would need a bone scan and a CAT scan to determine if the cancer had spread anywhere in my body. HOLY SHIT! Spread in my body?? That wasn't even a thought in my mind until this surgeon brought it up.

And so came the tears, and the biggest question of all: "Am I going to survive?" In fact, my mom had to finish that question for me. All that came out was, "Am I going to..." and I choked through the tears. I turned to my mom and she finished "survive," choking through her own tears. I knew this question would not be answered with a yes or no because the doctors really don't know, everyone is different. However, my surgeon was being nice and said, "Lots of women your age survive, and you can, too." Do you think that made me feel any better? NOPE! After the consult was over we all went into yet another tiny room so the surgeon could examine the goods. Let me tell you, just in the past five days many women in the medical field have seen and felt my left boob! Whatever dignity I had went out the door the minute I felt the lump in the shower that night. This visit wasn't over yet; my surgeon also wanted me to have a "fine needle biopsy" of the lymph nodes under my left arm. There's that word again... biopsy!!

The doctors set up the biopsy in a matter of minutes and the next thing I knew, I was lying on a table with an ultrasound tech over me, yet again. This time, a different doctor was poking very thin needles into my armpit and pulling out tissue from it, to determine if the cancer cells had gone into my lymph nodes as well. I'm sure all of this is very overwhelming to read. Can you imagine how I felt?

I had about four days in between the surgeon consult/needle biopsy and the bone/CAT scans. Another four days to worry about whether this cancer had spread to other parts of my body. Let me just tell you, the mind is a very powerful thing, and it can play tricks on you. I swear I felt like I was really. I had chest pains, which only made me think that the cancer had spread to my lungs. Four days, feeling like this was the end for me. As much as my family loves me, I know they were getting sick of hearing me tell them I was dying.

The day I had the bone and CAT scans was a long day. I had to stay at the hospital all day because when you have a bone scan they insert radioactive dye into your veins, but after they do that, you have to wait three-and-a-half hours until you can be scanned. The test really isn't bad except that the scan comes really close to your face and all I could think about was that it was going to break, fall on my face, and crush me to death. When it was over, the tech handed me a paper and said, "If you are going to the airport in the next two days, you will need this to get through the metal detectors." The paper stated that for medical reasons I had been given radioactive dye and I would be "radioactive" for the next two days. My sister jokingly asked me if I was going to glow in the dark. Ha Ha.

Two days after I had the bone and CAT scans, my surgeon called me. Now before the phone rang, I had reheated some pizza I had made the night before, got cozy into bed, and started eating and watching TV. For that hour before the phone rang I was totally fine, I hadn't thought of the cancer or if it had spread or anything about this hell. One hour out of four days. I picked up the phone and my surgeon told me that she had received the results of the bone/CAT scans, and that both scans were negative. NEGATIVE!! Finally, some good news!! The cancer had not spread to my bones or any organ in my body. Maybe things were looking up? The surgeon then explained that the results for the needle biopsy came back positive and the cancer cells had spread to my lymph nodes, but that they wouldn't know how many were affected until I went for the MRI. Let's just say, I wasn't able to finish my pizza after that.

Chapter 3

September 26, 2012

Do You Know What Breasts Are??

The past three weeks felt like an eternity. I had a mammogram, an ultrasound, a biopsy, been told I have breast cancer, had a bone scan, a cat scan and a needle biopsy, was scheduled for an MRI, had met with my now breast surgeon and was going to meet with my soon to be oncologist. As you can imagine, I had a different emotion every hour!

My boyfriend went with me to meet the oncologist. She was very nice, young, probably my age. Under different circumstances I think if we had just met on the street we would be friends. She and two of her PAs sat down and talked to my boyfriend and me about what the plan is for my treatment. My oncologist feels that since I do have cancer in the nodes, and since my tumors are "above average," that chemo should be the first step. She wants to shrink the tumors as much as possible with chemo first, then have surgery.

Chemo... this is what I fear the most. I've had small surgical procedures in the past and I went to school to be a surgical technologist so I've seen surgery, been right in the "meat" of it. I'm not scared of the surgery. I am so afraid to go through chemotherapy. The oncologist had to, of course, go through all the side effects and what chemotherapy would or could do to my body. She explained that I will start losing all my hair within the first month of chemo, so her advice was to cut my hair short to "lesson the blow." Okay, not too bad so far. I mean, I'm not going to have to worry about shaving my legs or anywhere else on my body for a while... wink wink. Looking at myself bald is going to take getting used to but if that was the worst thing that could happen I would be totally fine with this. I can also deal with the vomiting, but luckily my oncologist said I wouldn't be vomiting that much because they will give me lots of anti-nausea and vomiting meds. However, these meds have side effects. UGH!!

The oncologist said that sometimes chemotherapy can weaken the heart. I'm young, I'm really not worried about that. She stressed the fact that I will be very tired and some days won't feel like getting out of bed but that I have to exercise at least three times a week... does that make sense to you? I don't exercise now, someone may have to come to my house and physically move my legs for me. Chemo also stops your menstrual cycle, okay, now we're talkin'! That's a definite plus. I don't know a woman out there that would be upset to not have her period. Because (I'm doing it again) I have this estrogen receptor. I have to go on a pill every day for the next five years. I'm getting ahead of myself talking about that pill. I have to concentrate on chemotherapy first.

I decided to tell my daughters once I had all the information. This was not going to be easy. I'm going to pause now, and let you grab some tissues....

So one day, after my daughters got off the bus from school, I sat them down and I put my son, who is only a year old, on my lap and explained that I had something very important to tell them. I will never forget this conversation for as long as I live. I started with, "Do you know what breasts are?" Silly question maybe, but this is 2012, and I refer to breasts as something you eat off a chicken. Girls have boobs. They both looked up at me with their big blue eyes and shook their heads no. I explained that boobs are actually called breasts and that Mommy has breast cancer. Now, my daughter, Olivia, remembers that when she was five, her Papa (my dad) died of cancer. My daughter, Alaina, associates cancer with a pre-school teacher she had, Miss Mandy, who even after pre-school was over still stayed in touch with us and who has become such a wonderful friend to me. However, at the time Miss Mandy had breast cancer, Alaina was only three and doesn't really remember it. The minute I said cancer, Olivia started to cry, which made me cry, which then made Alaina cry. I tried to explain to them that I was going to be very sick for a while but that I would be better by next year. Okay, so a year to a child is like FOREVER! Kids have no concept of time, so trying to give them a timeline wasn't working. I also told them that I was going to lose my hair. Oh boy!

"You're going to be bald like Daddy?" YUP. Alaina, sitting in her chair across from me, pushed herself away from me in her chair. "I don't want to see you with no hair, you will look ugly." Well, children are honest, what could I say to that? Maybe I would look ugly? I told her I would wear a scarf so she wouldn't have to see my bald head. This kid is the funniest kid I've ever met, she doesn't mean or know that she's being funny, which just makes her even funnier. She looked at me with this what-are-you-stupid attitude and says, "What's a scarf gonna do for your head, scarves go around your neck!" I laughed so hard.

Olivia asked, "Who is going to take care of us when you're sick?" I told them that I would still be caring for them but that we might have a lot more visitors once I start my treatment. Olivia asked the BIG question... "Mommy... are you going to die?" (I told you to get a tissue)

"No girls, I am not going to die, I'm going to be very sick and look a little weird for a while but I am going to get better and be fine." That was the hardest question for me to answer because at that very minute, I was lying to my daughters. I have no idea if I'm going to live or die, or if I'm going to get better or not, but I couldn't tell them that... I couldn't tell them the truth. The truth is that their mom is so scared that she will not survive. The truth is that every time I take a shower I cry my eyes out because I have no control over this situation. The truth is that I'm a complete mess over this crappy hand that I was dealt! It would be so easy for me to just say SCREW THIS I'm not doing it, and I've thought about it so many times, but then I look at my kids and I want to see them grow up, I want to be there when they graduate and get married. I want to see my grandchildren someday, so as much as I want to throw in the towel, I won't. I will fight and I will survive for those three little faces.

Chapter 4

September 27, 2012

Another WTF Moment

At the consult with my oncologist, I will be honest, I didn't hear very much of that conversation. I heard all the negative side effects and that I needed to cut my hair. Everything in between that is pretty much a blur. When you have to listen to people who are bombarding you with a lot of information and a lot of it you can't even pronounce, let alone know the meaning of, it seems to me like your brain decides it's got all it can take and just concentrates on just a little bit of information. You are still listening to these people talk and shaking your head and answering them but you're not really processing it. That's why it is a good idea to bring someone with you.

My sister, Beth, came with me the night I had my hair cut. I knew I had to go through with it but I really didn't want to. I had pretty, shoulder-length hair. It took me a while to get it that length, and I wanted it to grow even longer. In fact, when my hairdresser, who is a long-time friend of Beth's, found out I was coming in for a short haircut, she was shocked. I didn't say too much while my hair was getting cut. I really didn't even want to look in the mirror. When my hairdresser was done, I just said thank you, hugged her, and we left. When Beth and I got to the car, I wanted to burst out in tears but I wasn't going to do that with her in the car. We are very emotional people. It's like a domino effect, if I started crying, Beth would have started, too, and I wasn't going to have us both sobbing in the car over my short hair... and well, it wasn't really about the hair.

I was scheduled to have an MRI and an echocardiogram on a Saturday, great way to start my weekend! The only good thing about having tests done on a weekend is that the hospital is pretty much a ghost town. I really didn't have to wait much at all. I had never had an echocardiogram before so I really didn't know what to expect.

Here is some info if you don't already know. An echocardiogram allows the doctors to see the heart beating, and to see the heart valves and other structures of the heart. It's pretty much an ultrasound of your heart.

The echo lasted about 25 minutes and then I was off to the MRI. MRIs make me nervous... I don't like being in tiny spaces and I really don't like having objects over my face. I've only had one MRI before, it was because I was having migraines, so when I had that MRI, the tech had me lie on my back with a cloth over my face and headphones on, then pushed me into this cylinder-shaped machine. I laid there, listening to music through the headphones until the test was over. They will also give you a "clicker" to push in case you need to get the tech's attention. The minute you push the clicker, the tech's voice comes through your headphones and asks if something is wrong.

This breast MRI was different. I had to lie on my stomach, face down, and put my boobs into two holes in the table of the machine. The tech pushed me in, with my headphones on and clicker in my hand. As I went into the machine I got very dizzy, but the tech assured me that the dizzy feeling would pass.

Okay, I was ready... I could do this and not freak out. All of a sudden, it got really hot, to the point where I was sweating. Oh no....

"Corey, are you okay?" I heard the tech's voice from my headphones.

"No, I'm going to throw up." The tech raced in the room and pulled me out of the MRI, sat me up and gave me a bedpan, which I mostly threw up in. Ever notice that when you are in the hospital and feel the urge to vomit, someone always brings you a bedpan, like one of those little pink plastic bean-shaped pans... you know what I mean? I don't know anyone who vomits in the shape of a bean. I don't have that talent, so it mostly got in the pan.

I knew I had to finish the MRI, this was the "test of all tests." My surgeon needed this completed to really see exactly how big my tumors are. Okay, back in I go! Luckily, I was fine for the rest of it. When it was all done, I still felt crummy but I was glad that all of the testing was over and we could start treating this horrible nightmare... or so I thought.

Three days after my MRI, I felt good. I wasn't even thinking about the MRI results, I was trying to stay positive about this crappy situation and was preparing myself for chemotherapy. Then the phone rang.... At least this time I wasn't eating. My surgeon was on the other end of the phone. It's never good news when she calls. She explained that the MRI showed my tumors to be much bigger than she had expected, and that there was "something" in a different quadrant of my left breast (the breast with the tumors, c'mon people stay with me). My surgeon explained that the "rule" is, if you have cancer in two or more quadrants of the same breast the surgeons remove the whole thing. She also said if I didn't care about "saving" the breast then she would just remove it and we wouldn't need another biopsy. She then told me that the MRI found "something" in the right breast, which we would need to biopsy. Another WTF moment. If I had any positive thoughts in my mind about this situation, they were all gone by the time I got off the phone with my surgeon... time for another biopsy!

Chapter 5

September 28, 2012

The Drama Sets In

It's been two days since I heard the results from the MRI. Let me explain my thoughts within those last two days....

I've had a cold for two weeks now. I knew I needed to go see a doctor and get it checked because I start chemo in seven days and I NEED to be healthy and strong for that. So, within these two weeks, I've pictured myself dying in the hospital because I started chemo, already sick, and now I'm not going to survive, all because of a cold! See, the mind tricks are at it again.

Two weeks ago, I woke up with this stupid cold and a sore throat and now it has turned into a respiratory infection. Are you kidding me?! I was put on a Z-pak for five days but this drug stays in your system for 10 days. I called my chemo nurse and asked her if I can still start chemo on the 4th. She said it was totally fine. The weird thing is, I'm very afraid of chemo but I really do want to do it and get it over with. It's like when you were in elementary school and you had to read your book report out loud. No one wanted to be the first one to read it, but the smart kids knew that if they were the first to read it to the class, they could make eye contact with the teacher for the rest of the class without sweating and quickly looking down in their desk pretending to be busy so they wouldn't be called on... I only know this because I was not that smart kid.

A few months after I had my son, I was a little depressed and just didn't feel right. I know what you're thinking... post-partum depression, but that's not what I had. A midwife I had seen when I was pregnant with him told me that behind every great woman is a great therapist. (I only saw midwives with all of my pregnancies, it's not a religious thing and I definitely had an epidural with all three of my children, but I just feel midwives spend more time with you than the doctors do.) I didn't really want to go to a therapist. I thought I could "heal" myself. My dad always told me, mind over matter. I was also a little embarrassed about going to talk to a "shrink." I learned quickly that I was wrong and there is no shame in going to talk to someone. The therapist I went to see is a lovely woman. She gave me a lot of insight into "healing" myself and thinking positively. I went to her for a few months and then she and I both decided my attitude all around was much better than the first day I walked into her office, and I really didn't need any more sessions.

Anyone who knows me knows I am a very negative person. I have been this way all my life. I know bad things happen to good people, but when they keep happening it's very hard to be positive about anything. When I got diagnosed with breast cancer, I called my therapist and told her to sign me up again. When I walked back into her office, saw her and sat down and talked with her, I felt better. She agreed with me that this situation sucks then she asked, "What can you do about it?"

My response to that question was "Nothing." I have no control over this situation so no, I can't do anything, this just sucks. This is NEGATIVE Corey talking. POSITIVE Corey would have said... Of course I can do something. I can smile every day, I can laugh every day, I can say this does suck but things could be a lot worse for me, I am going to go through hell but I will beat this. POSITIVE Corey doesn't always like to come out and play.

The day before I got the results about the MRI, I had gone to see my therapist again. I was feeling good, I was emotionally okay, and was ready for the next step... which I thought was chemotherapy. The next day, still feeling good, mind you, that damn phone rang. Which just goes to show I should never answer the phone. I was on the phone for seven minutes and thirteen seconds. In seven minutes, I went from feeling like everything was going to be okay to now I'm not so sure if anything will be okay. After I hung up the phone, I broke down in tears. Why is this happening to me?! I called my boyfriend but he didn't answer. I called Beth but she didn't answer, either. I called my brother, David, but he didn't answer, either. Why isn't anyone answering the damn phone when I need to talk to them!? In that very moment, I felt like I was all alone... I wanted to die.

Dramatic! I know.

Chapter 6

October 2, 2012

Bad Luck

I am a stay-at-home mom. Some people have told me, "That is the hardest job in the world," while others have said, "You don't work, you just stay home with the kids all day." I actually do a lot more than "stay home with the kids all day." I do laundry every day. I dust, which, let me just tell you and my mom can vouch for this, I hate to do, but it has to be done so I grin and bear it. I cook all the meals, I make breakfast and lunches for the girls before school and for my boyfriend before he goes to work all day. I make the bottles, and feed Landon, my son. I wash the floors once a week and vacuum every day. I also clean the bathroom and kitchen daily, and I'm also the dishwasher. I do all the food shopping, and take the kids to every appointment they have. I also get up with Landon twice a night, because for some reason this child doesn't want me to sleep... ever. I am a busy girl and this cancer crap has thrown a monkey-wrench into my life. I have been told from many different people that chemo wipes you out, that you are so exhausted that you don't feel like doing anything. I have three kids who need me, a house that needs to be clean, clothes that need to be washed, and dinner that needs to be made. This is my job, and I am damn good at it. I know I will have good days, I just need to keep focused on that... ugh.

I started making "chemo food." Beth bought me the cancer-fighting cookbooks so I looked through them, sticky-noted the recipes I wanted to make and freeze, and my mom brought over all the ingredients I needed. I only made three things, each of them had over 10 ingredients and it took me a long time to make them. I felt I needed to make these things, for myself, so that I wouldn't need to bother anyone to make them for me. I hate the thought of being someone's burden and it kills me to have to depend on people. I know, you're all saying, "You're not burdening anyone," and that may be true, but this is how I feel. I have gone shopping every day since last Friday, to get extra stuff like shampoo and body soap, detergents, and frozen foods. I'm really trying to make this chemo crap easy on everyone, even though we all know there will be nothing "easy" about it.

I have talked to a lot of people about breast cancer, either they themselves have had it or someone they know had it. This kinda makes me feel good? I say that as a question because I guess I'm not sure if it does or not. I feel good when I hear someone say, "I had it and I survived," or "I know someone who had it and it's been 15+ years and they are doing great." But it's still in the back of my head that I could die. My dad told me a few times that I was the strong one out of his kids, I'm guessing mentally because David definitely has me physically beat. I have thought and thought about why I had to get cancer, so maybe my dad was right. I was the one to get cancer because I am the strong one and I will fight it... either that or it's just plain shit luck! I consider myself a religious person, I was brought up a Baptist, went to Sunday school every Sunday when I was a kid, I do read the Bible from time to time and I pray a lot. I have prayed so many times for answers to everything. My dad was a very religious man; he read the Bible cover to cover. My dad would say, ask and you shall receive. Now, I don't think my dad meant ask God for a fancy new car or a million dollars and POOF it will appear. I do believe that if you do ask questions they will be answered, I just don't think I was "listening" to the answers. Maybe God gave me those answers, put them right in front of me several times, and I just didn't want to hear them. So, I feel like this cancer crap will give me all the answers I want. This is "make it or break it." I will find out who my real friends are by going through this, and maybe this will show me what exactly I want to do in life. I could be very wrong about all of this but right now, I need to think there is a better reason for this than just bad luck.

* * * *

That day my surgeon called me, when I was being very dramatic (remember?), she explained that the MRI had shown some "other spots" and that I needed another biopsy.

There are really no words to describe how I was feeling. I had all sorts of emotions going on. What do you think that does to a person, mentally and physically? I think it makes you stressed, and what happens when you get so stressed to the point of no return? I believe you get sick, you get migraines or headaches, you get aches and pains... you get cancer. (This is purely my own opinion)

Chapter 7

October 3, 2012

Maybe?

The emotions have set in and I am so angry. The past week has been a roller coaster ride from hell. I really feel like I'm going toe to toe with the devil himself!

I was scheduled for a biopsy yesterday. No problem, it's not my favorite test but I've done it before and I can do it again. This biopsy is to find out if the "something" they found in another part of my left breast and the "something" they found in my right breast are actually cancerous as well.

Once I got there, I was told this biopsy was going to be MRI-guided. Now remember, the last time I had an MRI, I had a cold and once they put me in the machine I got very dizzy and threw up in the plastic bean. I still have a cold. So, when they got me all set and pushed me into the machine, what do you think happened? I got very dizzy and threw up in the plastic bean!! The doctor that was going to do the biopsy explained that this time I was going to have to be pulled in and out of the MRI several times to do the biopsy and since I was getting sick, they wouldn't be able to do it. I would have to reschedule. Okay, reschedule me, no problem.

Big problem! My surgeon's PA called me this morning and said, "I'm so sorry to hear that you couldn't have the biopsy, but unfortunately you won't be able to start chemotherapy tomorrow."

WHAT!!!!!??! The PA explained that my oncologist needs the results of the biopsy in order to make my chemo "cocktail." I cannot express the anger that I feel right now. I actually told the PA to have my surgeon call me because I want to ask her how long I have to live without going through chemo and surgery. I haven't even started this and I'm ready to call it quits! I have said before, I am very scared of the chemo, but I want to do it, I want this over and done with. While I was talking to the PA on the phone, I told her my concerns. We are now pushing chemo back probably another two weeks, so in the next two weeks I get to worry that my tumors are getting bigger and the cancer is spreading?!?! Not something I want to do!!

I'm supposed to be positive through all of this, that's what everyone keeps telling me. I keep telling myself, everything happens for a reason... right? Maybe this is a good thing, I still have this head cold so my immune system isn't up to par, and if I were to have chemo on top of this head cold maybe I would be worse. Maybe this is God's way of telling me to get some better antibiotics so I can kick this cold, get stronger, and beat this devil down!

Chapter 8

October 5, 2012

Anger and Rage

I was told there are emotional stages of breast cancer (maybe all kinds of illness, really):

- Denial and Shock
- Anger and Rage
- Stress and Depression
- Grief and Fear
- Acceptance and Adjustment
- Fight and Hope

I'm not sure if these are in the right order, I definitely felt the denial and shock, yes 100% this is no way happening to me. Once I was over the shock, I went straight to the grief and fear. How do you not fear the unknown? I could die, my kids could lose their mommy. We aren't talking about going to a haunted house and getting scared when Michael Myers jumps out at you. I'm talking about death, and it's scary. It's scary for me, a 30-year-old with three kids, which just brings me back to the denial and shock stage... this can't be happening to me. Last night I hit anger and rage straight on. Oh yeah, this shit gets better....

Yesterday I asked the PA to have my surgeon call me. I am just so frustrated with all of this, my emotions are all over the place. I was ready to start chemo on Thursday, so when they said I couldn't start until I had the MRI biopsy, I was so upset I wanted to talk to my surgeon, one on one. She called me late last night. So far I like my surgeon. I have heard from many people that this surgeon is one of the best, which makes me want to stay with her. I explained to her that when I went for the biopsy, I got very dizzy and nauseated so the tech and doctor that were performing this didn't want to go on with the biopsy.

"Is there any other way to do this biopsy?" NOPE! My surgeon said this is the only way to know for sure if the other "something" in my breasts is cancerous. Unless I don't want to know for sure, then they will move on with the chemo and hope for the best. Obviously, I want to know if both of my boobs are trying to kill me. She also said I should take a Xanax to relax so I can complete the biopsy. Hold up... wait a minute. This is NOT all in my head!! I do have a history of anxiety, and I am claustrophobic, but I have been in an MRI before this cancer bullshit even happened. I took a Xanax and I was fine. I also took a Xanax for the MRI the time before last, and I got very dizzy and nauseated. So again, this is not all made up in my head!

I'm getting dizzy and sick either because I have a cold or because of the high-powered MRI. My surgeon really wasn't hearing me, though. She was preoccupied, she kept telling me she was in the car, getting lost. I get it, doctors have lives, too. She asked me to try the MRI biopsy again, and if I get sick again then we won't waste any more time and we will move forward with the chemo. I agreed to try it again. I was assured I would be in a lesser-powered MRI and that it shouldn't make me dizzy, but that I should also take the Xanax to calm my nerves.

I cannot tell you how angry I was when I got off the phone with her. I did have a few tears, but mostly I was just mad. I wanted to fight someone, I wanted to punch big holes in the walls. My daughter asked me what was wrong, and I just said, "Nothing, I stubbed my toe." Could I show my anger? No, I had to hold it in. I wanted to scream so badly but I couldn't, because at the end of the day I'm still a mom and I wasn't going to scream and yell, or break things. So, I went in the shower and I cried, which brought me back to grief and fear, which turned full circle back into denial and shock. This is not really happening to me!!

Chapter 9

October 9, 2012

Cruel Joke

Anxiety is a strange thing. In the dictionary anxiety means a psychological and physiological state characterized by emotional, cognitive, and behavioral components. It is the displeasing feeling of fear and concern.

I think I have had anxiety my whole life; in fact, I believe (and I could be very wrong) that anxiety is hereditary. I blame my dad for this; he had anxiety through the roof! My daughter Olivia, who has anxiety even at only eight years old, will blame me for it someday, too.

It has been seven days since I got the bad news, that because I wasn't able to have the MRI biopsy, I couldn't start chemo. These past seven days have felt like an eternity! After I talked to my surgeon, I was angry and upset for maybe two days. Over the weekend, I felt calm... which is very weird because I don't know how to be calm. I don't even know how to relax. Every day, since I talked to my surgeon, I woke up and said to myself, "You're not going to think about the cancer today." It seems a little silly, and really didn't work throughout the day, but I said it every morning. I don't want to think about this anymore. I want to have fun-filled days with my kids without getting depressed about this, because it is always on my mind.

Tomorrow I go back to the hospital and try the MRI biopsy again, and the anxiety has taken over me. Anxiety is like a cruel joke. My primary care physician once told me that anxiety manifests itself in so many different ways, once you get used to it in one part of your body it says... "Wait a minute, you know why you're feeling this way? Okay, I'm gonna take over a different spot in your body now, ha ha!" From tingling in my hands and feet to migraines, I have had every sort of feeling that can stem from anxiety. Just thinking about how I have to go back and complete this MRI gives me a headache. Maybe some people have anxiety that comes and goes and can be controlled, but I think mine is constantly tormenting me. I've tried meditation... oh boy, that just makes me even more anxious. Prescription medications, like Xanax, helps a lot because they help me sleep. I've tried calming foods and lotions, what a joke. I was eating better and smelled good, though. I have come to the conclusion that anxiety is just a part of who I am, and I have to accept it.

Remember how I told you there are emotional stages of breast cancer? I think I have hit another one. Acceptance and Adjustment. I do wake up every day and hope that this is just a nightmare. I can pretend all day, every day, that it's not really happening to me. Then reality sets in, this is real, it's happening. I have to accept it and adjust to it, just like my anxiety. I've got breast cancer, so bring it on, I'm ready to beat this thing!

Chapter 10

October 12, 2012

A Very Long Day

I made it through the MRI biopsy on Wednesday, woohoo! I had to take a Xanax so Beth drove me to the hospital. The Xanax did help, but I think being in the lesser-powered magnet helped as well, and instead of having my head straight down I asked the techs if I could lay my head to the side. I ended up with a stiff neck but getting this test done was worth it. Beth was also able to come in the room with me when the doctors were performing the biopsy. Even though I couldn't touch her or see her, just knowing she was there made me feel better. We were there the whole day, it took a very long time but now it's done and over with, and no matter what the outcome is, chemotherapy starts next week.

CAUTION I'm going to get graphic....

I can't really tell you step by step what was happening through the MRI biopsy. I couldn't see anything. The doctor starts off by numbing the area, and honestly, I think that hurts more than anything. "Little burn, little pinch," that's what they tell you once they insert the needles. Little burn? NOPE! Big burn, and big pinch! Once the doctor thought I was all numbed up she started the biopsy. This doctor used a vacuum-assisted needle (I don't know what that is, either). I could hear what sounded like power tools on the side of me. Ummm, I'm pretty sure I came here for a biopsy, not a tune-up! It's scary enough going through a biopsy, but not being able to see what was happening scared me even more. The doctor was able to get the tissue samples on the right breast, then it was time to do it all over again on the left breast. Once she was done, I was able to turn over on my back and the two techs held gauze tightly on the areas that had just been "drilled." After I had stopped bleeding, they wheeled me up to get another mammogram. The doctor that had performed the biopsy also put one marker in both my breasts. I had markers put in when I had the ultrasound-guided biopsy. It's just so if they need to do surgery, the doctors know exactly where they are going. When I got home from the hospital, the Xanax hadn't worn off and I was still really tired. I was also very numb. The doctor must have put a lot of numbing meds on the area. After the second time I told her I could still feel the needles going into my breasts, she must have doubled the dose. The techs had informed us that once I left the hospital, I wasn't to do any lifting over five pounds, because my incisions could start bleeding again. I have a one-year-old, who is 21 pounds and doesn't walk. I am going to pick him up and carry him when I need to, I just don't have any other option.

A few hours had passed and I started bleeding again. Beth ran to CVS and bought gauze and changed the dressings for me. I put ice and pressure on my breasts the rest of the night, which stopped the bleeding completely. The next night, I took a shower. I took off the gauze, but I was told I needed to let the little Steri-Strips, like tiny bandages, fall off on their own. I can't even describe how bad my boobs look. Battle wounds! At this point, the surgeon may as well remove them both, because they will never look the same after this anyway!

Waiting for the results wasn't as bad this time. I mean, I know what the outcome is. I have breast cancer, I need chemo, surgery, and radiation. That isn't going to change. The fine details might shift a bit but I know what needs to happen. The PA called me this morning to give me the results. My right breast is benign, no cancer, good news! So, at least I know only my left boob is trying to kill me.

I looked at myself in the mirror for a long time today, I never thought this would ever happen to me. I had a friend a few years back who told me she was actually waiting to develop breast cancer. Breast cancer ran deep in her family. I can remember thinking to myself, thank God that will never happen to me, I will never have breast cancer, I don't have a family history of it. Just goes to show, never say never!

A lovely woman I met recently, a breast cancer survivor, told me her doctor said to her, "History has to start somewhere." That plays over and over in my head. In less than twenty years my two little girls will be having mammograms and MRIs to see if they will develop breast cancer, too... because of me. In twenty years, there better be a cure for this breast cancer shit, because if not, God help those doctors who have to deal with me going through this horrible ordeal with one of my daughters.

Chapter 11

October 16, 2012

A Close Fourth

Have you ever watched *Parenthood*? The show, not the movie with Steve Martin. I just started watching a couple of weeks ago, not sure what season I'm on but so far the main storyline is breast cancer. One of the characters, a young mom of three, was just diagnosed. Hmmmm... that sounds familiar. To sum up the last three episodes, her character had a mammogram, went to meet her surgeon, found out she has a very small tumor in one of her breasts, was told she would need surgery, and at the very end of the last show she told her family what was going on. This is over three weeks, which in television time is probably one week's time. This aggravates me. Firstly, it doesn't happen this way, definitely not that quickly. As we all know now, there is extensive testing that has to be done before this woman can have surgery. Secondly, just surgery? No chemo? Radiation? That wasn't even discussed, although I'm getting ahead of myself. Maybe in the next episode they will talk about it. Lastly, I'm sure this character will be diagnosed, tested, treated, and cured in a three-month period. Again, television time. I get that the writers can't show a whole year of this character going through breast cancer, who wants to see that? Well, who wants to live that!? If this were television time and I was going to only have cancer for three months, I wouldn't complain. Sign me up! That's not realistic, I really do love the show though, I mean who doesn't love Dax Shepard?!

The past few days have been... well, not that great. When I got diagnosed with breast cancer, I thought all the other drama in my life would just move aside or disappear. I was very wrong. Having family, siblings in particular, means there is always some sort of drama. My girls go see their dad on the weekends, drama. My girls are almost two years apart, and they fight constantly... DRAMA! I'm in a relationship... which eventually leads to (and we all get it at some point in our relationships) DRAMA. I really thought that cancer would trump all the other bullshit in my life. Maybe it should, but it doesn't. Everyone keeps telling me that I have to put myself first. This is difficult for me. Fifteen years ago, oh hell, yeah, I would have said, "Of course this is all about me and I will put myself first!" Things are different now. Once I had Olivia, at 22 years old and not knowing what to do with a baby, I had to grow up and put her first. Now I have three little people I have to put before me, so maybe I won't be first but I will be a close fourth.

I start chemotherapy on Thursday, two days away and I'm getting very nervous. I woke up at 3 a.m. because I swore I was having a heart attack. I had such bad chest pains, which then turned into a burning sensation. I'm chalking it up to heartburn, or as I say in Italian, *agita*. I did have pie and ice cream before I went to bed last night... Don't judge.

I am a nervous person. That's not going to change, and I know that the "heart attack" I was having last night was just anxiety. I keep telling myself, chemo's not going to be that bad. My dad always told me, "Mind over matter," and I do believe that. I have been through a lot in a short period of time. Married, divorced, I've given birth three times, I lost three people who were close to me, I've been in destructive relationships, and I know what it feels like to be physically and mentally sick. I know that I will have good and bad days, but I told myself that for this one year I am only going to think positive, and surround myself with positive people. So... if you're not a positive person or at least not good at pretending you are, then I can't talk to you for at least another year. Sorry.

Chapter 12

September 25, 2012

No Turning Back Now

I give my first chemo experience a B-, and I'm being generous. Before we go right to the chemo, I have to tell you about my port. You have to read this part in a British accent, it just sounds better... A port is a small medical appliance that is placed beneath the skin. A catheter connects the port to a vein under the skin. The port has a septum through which medication can be injected and blood can be drawn many times. Now re-read it in English. A port is a small medical appliance that is placed beneath the skin. A catheter connects the port to a vein under the skin. The port has a septum through which medication can be injected and blood can be drawn many times. See, sounds way better in a British accent!

Prior to my visit, I was given instructions, the dos and don'ts. A big don't for me was "You many not eat or drink anything after 6 a.m. the day of your port procedure." AHHHHH!!!! My port wasn't scheduled to be put in until 12:00 that afternoon. Okay, I may be thin, but I eat a lot. I need to eat or else I will get nauseated, and if you ask my mom, she will tell you I need to eat to control my moods. Growing up, my mom used to tell my high school boyfriends that would pick me up at the house, "Make sure you feed her." Wicked embarrassing at the time but now I see it.

Thursday, I set my alarm to wake up at 5 a.m. so I could at least eat a little something. I ended up eating half of a muffin and then went back to bed. My boyfriend took me to the hospital around 11:30 a.m. There was a lot of prepping before the actual procedure could take place, so I had to get there a half-hour earlier. He and I met the PA once we got in the hospital, and the PA took us up to the right floor and chatted with us a little before the nurse took me in for the procedure. This was it. There was no turning back now.

When I was all prepped and on the table, the doctor came in to introduce himself and explain exactly what he was going to be doing. I love information but at that very moment, I wished he hadn't told me. It just made me more anxious. The nurse was very nice, she even held my hand. The doctor assured me that this procedure was not going to hurt me at all. "We are going to give you lots of drugs, lovely patient, so if you feel anything, you tell me and I will give you more drugs, okay?" He was funny, but he meant it. I started to cry. He stopped and said "More drugs!" I was awake for this procedure but he gave me a relaxant, and at one point I thought I could go right to sleep. The procedure took about an hour and a half. They cleaned me up, my PA met me in that room, and took me back upstairs where my boyfriend was waiting for me and took me in for chemo. At this point I was wicked tired and hungry, and yes, Mom, grumpy. The PA must have been in cahoots with my mom or saw that I was getting angry because she ran to get me a tuna sandwich and a soda. I was very thankful for that.

Okay, here it comes, definitely can't run now. I had to sit in a recliner and my boyfriend sat in a chair across from me. The meds the port doctor gave me must have been wearing off, because I was in pain. The nurse gave me some Tylenol to take the edge off. We sat in this little tiny "pod," that's what they call the chemo rooms. It's almost like a cubicle at an office, but there is a curtain in the doorway to block out the hall. Before the nurse brought in the chemo, I asked to use the bathroom. I closed and locked the door behind me. I looked in the mirror at my chest and saw the gauze covering a big bulge with a needle and wire hanging out of it. I lost it, dropped to my knees and cried. This was it, time to get poisoned and I was scared. At that moment, I wished I could have snapped my fingers and had my mom, dad, grandparents, and all my siblings there with me. I put some water on my face to calm down the redness. I came out of the bathroom and got right back in the recliner. I was as ready as I would ever be.

The nurse came in with IV fluids first to "drown my kidneys." After that was complete, the nurse took out the chemo. The first one was in a huge syringe, and the chemo inside it was red. The nurse had to sit there with me for ten minutes and dispense it herself. After that was done, I really had to pee. I went into the bathroom, wheeling my IV stand with me. I sat down and peed bright orange... well, that's not something you see every day. The color was from the red dye in the chemo I had just been given. The nurse said it shouldn't last more than a couple of days. I sat back down in the recliner for the second chemo treatment - this one was a bag hooked up to my port. It would take a little over an hour to be finished. I flipped on the TV but there weren't any good channels and nothing on to watch, so my boyfriend and I played cards for the remaining time. Everyone looks at me funny when they see a deck of cards in my pocketbook; well, it just goes to show, you never know when you're gonna need them. Once I was all done, I had to wait for the nurse to come and remove the needle from my port and put a new dressing on it. I was instructed to drink a lot, have small meals throughout the day, and that I should drink Ensure... yuck! I was also told I need to come back the next day to get a booster shot, to bring up my white cell count, since the chemo will be destroying all my cells, good and bad.

Before we went home, we stopped at Panera to get me an iced green tea. This might sound weird but I don't like liquids, especially water. My body really doesn't need to drink water every day. I'm sorta like a camel, I will go two days without drinking a thing, but the third day I will make up for it and drink a lot. My weakness is iced green tea from Panera. A while back, one of my friends introduced me to Panera's iced green tea, and I have been hooked ever since! When we got home, Mom and Beth were getting the kids ready for bed. My girls looked at my bandaged-up port and asked what it was. I explained as much as I could, but I was still a little groggy from the meds the port doctor had given me, and my mouth felt like it was full of marbles. When Mom and Beth left, my boyfriend and I ate the beef stew that had been cooking in the crockpot all day, that I had prepared before we left that morning to go to the hospital. I know what you're thinking, but I was shooting for normalcy. I was instructed to take the anti-nausea pills given to me after chemo. Ten minutes after I ate and took that pill, my heart started pounding and racing. I thought my heart was going to explode. I decided to call the on-call oncologist. He was very nice and reassured me that my heart wasn't going to explode and that 100 beats a minute is actually normal, that if it goes higher than 120 beats a minute that's a sign for concern. He also said that as long as I didn't have a fever I should be fine. I felt a little better after talking to him. My heart was still racing but I laid down on my left side and fell asleep. At 2:30 that morning I woke up very nauseated. I didn't know if I could take another anti-nausea pill because the medication instructions didn't say anything about what to do if I woke up sick in the middle of the night, and I wasn't about to call the on-call doc again. I got up, ate some saltines, choked down some water, and made peppermint tea. That seemed to help get me back to sleep. I felt a little sick in the morning, but I ate a bran muffin and had some hot green tea, and I also ate a prune. I wanted to make sure I could go to the bathroom before I took the anti-nausea meds. I'm sorry but if any of you have ever been constipated in your life, you know how awful it is. The number-one side effect of the nausea meds is constipation and by dammit, I will not get constipated!

Chapter 13

October 20, 2012

Not-So-Fast-Paced Corey

You gain strength, courage and confidence by every experience in which you really stop to look fear in the face.

- Eleanor Roosevelt

The morning after I had my first chemotherapy, I got out of bed, ate, and took my meds. Beth knocked on my door. The night before, I had told my mom and Beth that I would be fine to get the girls up and put them on the bus in the morning. Boy, was I happy to see Beth! Of course, I didn't let her know that. As she walked in the door, I said "I told you I would be fine to get the kids on the bus." She said, "I know, I was just checking." She always knows when to check up on me. Truth is, I knew either my mom or Beth would be at my door that morning. Beth said, "Well, since you're fine, I guess I will get to work." Was this statement a set-up? My response was, "The bus will be here any minute, so you might as well just put them on the bus." I hadn't had time to get dressed or put makeup on, and there was no way I was going outside without putting my face on first.

I am usually a fast-paced person. On a normal day, I can get up, get dressed, put full make-up on, do the dishes, and clean up the kitchen all in one hour before the girls wake up in the morning. I like to get everything done early so I don't have to do it throughout the day. I have a feeling fast-paced Corey has left the building. I didn't get dressed or even think about make-up until 11 a.m. that morning. I made myself an egg, and, surprisingly, I was drinking a lot of liquids. Getting the baby in and out of the tub and the high chair was tough. Every time I moved, it felt as though my port was ripping out of my chest. I took the baby for a walk around 1 p.m., just up and down the street. I'm really trying to do everything the doctors are telling me to do, including exercise. My mom came to the house when the girls got off the bus, not to check up on me... well, probably to check up on me but she was there to take me to the hospital to get my booster shot.

We packed up the kids and got to the hospital around 4 p.m. The nurse was very nice, and was asking me how I was feeling after chemo. I told her I felt like there was an endless pit in my stomach. She asked if I could elaborate. I said, "I don't know how to describe it, my stomach just feels gross." I think she understood. I did have questions, though.

"Why am I flushed in the face?" She explained that my face felt that way because of the chemo and it would go away, which it did.

"What do I do in the middle of the night when I wake up sick to my stomach?" She said (and I'm cringing even typing this out), "Did you take the suppository?" If you've ever been constipated, you know what a suppository is. My response was "No." The nurse looked at me, shaking her head and said, "You need to take that before you go to bed; it will last in your system all night." I said okay, but I know full well that unless I am physically unable to lift my head off the floor, there is no way in hell I'm going to shove that up my rear! My other question was, "I gained four pounds in a day?" The nurse said, "Oh yes, that's all the sodium we gave you with the chemo, it will flush its way out of you." Ugh....

2:30 a.m. came once again, and I woke up sick to my stomach. That's right, I didn't take the suppository. I ate some crackers and had a few sips of water, then I felt a little better and fell back asleep. This morning I felt pretty good, I didn't need to take any meds. I made myself an egg and a pretty gross shake made up of Ensure, frozen strawberries, bran and flaxseed. That's right, more bran... no way this chick is getting constipated. I took the kids for a short walk, it was such a beautiful day. Fast-paced Corey can stay under wraps for a while, this not-so-fast-paced Corey now has time to stop and smell the roses.

Chapter 14

October 24, 2012

And on the Sixth Day...

It has been six days since I first had chemo. Six long days. I am keeping extensive notes every day on my overall health since chemo. Saturday night was another really bad night. I woke up two or three times that night, each time sick to my stomach. Again, I did not use the suppository, I just refuse to do it. I can get through the sickness with crackers and water. I woke up Sunday morning very tired. That whole day I felt sick, had heartburn, was very bloated, my mouth felt like it had marbles in it, and I was extremely hungry, and eating all day. It didn't matter what I put in my stomach - water, crackers, potatoes - everything I ate just made me feel sick, but my stomach was growling like I was hungry. It's a weird feeling, the only thing I can compare it to is being pregnant. When I was pregnant, I ate all the time, but felt sick all the time as well. That night I took a Xanax before I went to sleep. I actually slept most of the night; in fact, I didn't wake up sick to my stomach. I did wake up once that night but it was because I had a headache.

Monday morning, I got up and did my usual routine. I got lunches ready, got my face on and got dressed, and prepared something for the girls to eat for breakfast. The girls got on the bus and I talked to my neighbors for a few minutes. Landon ran out of formula, and because this child has a milk allergy, I can't just open the fridge and grab the 2% milk, he has to stay on "special" formula until he's 18 months old. So, I went to the market before 9 a.m., and got back pretty quickly. At this point, I really don't want to be out in the stores, or in crowds. I pick up every little cold, every virus out there when my immune system isn't compromised, now that it is compromised I'm afraid if I do get a cold or a virus I won't be able to fight it off. When I got back home I felt like I was going to pass out. I had a headache all day, my stomach was upset, and I had heart palpitations ALL day, which are just annoying. I noticed I really wasn't drinking anything, either, so I'm sure that contributed to most of my problems. In the middle of the day I took Landon for a walk, but I couldn't even make it all the way down my street this time. I had to turn around and go back home. I took a Xanax again before I went to bed and it seemed to make me sleep pretty well. It was the first time in four nights that I didn't get up in the middle of the night sick or with a headache.

Yesterday, I got up, did my whole routine, got lunches together, made breakfast, put my face on and got dressed. I put the girls on the bus and made breakfast for myself. I was feeling better but my heart was racing all day and I still had the palpitations. I just felt really sluggish. I attempted to take Landon for a walk but I just couldn't, I really didn't have the energy, so we just sat outside for a little while.

I have heard about all sorts of alternative healing and other options for combatting nausea instead of the anti-nausea meds. Don't get me wrong, I still plan on taking the meds. I just want to be aware of my options, in case I really can't take these meds anymore. I read about chiropractic and cancer, I've also been told acupuncture helps out with nausea from the chemo. Bottom line, my health insurance doesn't cover either of these but the chiropractor is cheaper, so I went to him. I'm not so sure he can help me, but my mom asked me to give it a try, so I will go a couple more times and see if it helps any. Last night I took a Xanax before bed and I slept pretty good. I did wake up in the middle of the night but it was because Landon woke up crying, not because I was feeling sick.

I'm Still Here

Today is a good day! I am so happy that I can say that. My heart is still racing and I am tired but I feel good for the first time in six days!! I will keep taking notes every day and compare with my next chemo treatment. It seems like days three, four, and five after chemo were the worst days for me. It also seems like the Monday after chemo (I have chemo on Thursdays) is the absolute worst day for me.

Some days there won't be a song in your heart. Sing anyway.

~Emory Austin

Chapter 15

October 31, 2012

Negativity Strikes Again!

Eight days ago I reached a turning point. I felt good. I have been so happy about these last eight days because now I know there is a light at the end of the tunnel. No matter how bad I feel those three days after chemotherapy, I know I will be feeling better. I have chemo coming up soon, and I'm getting nervous again. I'm hoping that this nervous feeling will eventually go away and I won't be worried and nervous every time I have to go back for treatments. I feel as though I get nervous over little, stupid things. I'm worried about what I will be able to eat, what I won't be able to eat. In fact, I was going to go totally bland two days before chemo and two days after chemo to see if it helped with the nausea. Bland is gross. Beth brought over my favorite candy bars yesterday. I told her about my bland diet and that I couldn't eat them for a while. Then last night as I was sitting in bed watching television, I thought to myself, I may not be able to eat anything pretty soon. I'm getting those candy bars in now while I still have taste buds to taste them, damn it!

The few days after chemotherapy, I really felt awful, I kept thinking to myself that it would get better. I kept pushing myself because I will not just lie down and die. If you were to tell me (and I have been told this) that during chemo all I was going to do is lie on the couch all day, not eat anything, just be tired and miserable, and I'm sure there are people going through chemo who can't do much of anything except lie on the couch, I'm not trying to offend anyone, everyone heals in their own way. However, in my mind, I'm thinking there is no way I'm going to do that. I am a stubborn girl, if you tell me I can't do something, I'm going to do it, and I'm going to make sure I do it better than you. If you tell me how I'm going to feel and I don't agree, I'm going to prove you wrong. Bottom line is this - everybody is different. I think I handled the first chemo treatment pretty well. It sucked, and I have been told that it will just get worse as the chemo builds up in my body. I know now though, that I just have to get through a few awful days to get to the good ones. It's like anything in life, you work hard to get something you want. I had eight really good days, so now when I do feel crappy, I just have to push through.

I definitely think attitude is more than half the battle in these situations. I can totally see why some people give up when they have cancer. I've only been through one treatment and already I never want to do it again. There are lots of people in the world who are very positive about their lives. I think that's awesome, I'm just not one of those people. I have always been a negative person, from as far back as I can remember. I have an idea why. My dad was negative about the world. He taught me to fear, not to trust, he made me very aware that the world is not all hearts and flowers. My dad's famous words were "Misery loves company."

My mom is different, though. She sees the good in people, she knows the world is not all great and bad things do happen to good people, but she still tries to see the positive side. I loved my dad, we were very close, but I should have taken after my mom. I have said before, I have had so many negative things happen to me - divorce, I lost both my grandparents who were very close to me. I lost my dad who was my protector and who I knew loved me more than anything. Do you know what it's like to be so consumed with grief and negativity that you can't see the positive in life? I do!

I have a beautiful family, and good friends. I should be counting my blessing every day. Instead, I'm constantly sad and worried every time my little girls go out the door that something awful is going to happen to them. That if I'm in a good relationship and am truly happy, that something bad will happen to us. I honestly believe this is why I have cancer. This is God's way of telling me, you got one more chance, start loving life or it will be taken from you. I *learned* to be negative, so now I have no choice but to reteach myself to be positive. Everyone has told me that attitude is 90% of the battle, so I have no choice but to invoke Positive Polly.

Chapter 16

November 3, 2012

Now It's Real

My boyfriend took me to the Cancer Center for my second chemo treatment, and as we walked up the stairs, I said "Okay, I'm ready to get poisoned." This is really how I feel. I have cancer, but I don't feel sick until I go get chemo. How crazy is this, the cancer isn't making me feel awful but the treatment for me to actually get better is what is making me sick. You know what else sounds crazy to me? I am getting treated for Breast Cancer the exact same way as someone who had it ten years ago. You're telling me that with all the donations and money towards research that in the past two years they weren't able to come up with something better than this horrible chemotherapy?! I'm back to the angry stage again.

My emotions are crazy these days. I was brushing Olivia's hair in the bathroom and she said, "Mommy, do you think Papa knows you have cancer in Heaven?" So, because it hurts me to talk about my dad to my kids I simply said, "I don't know, Livvy." When she left the bathroom, the tears started to come down my face. My boyfriend came in and asked what was wrong but I just , "Nothing, I'm fine." It's hard for me to tell him that I'm crying because I miss my dad. My boyfriend never met my dad, never got to see how close we really were. I feel that anyone who never met my dad wouldn't understand how sad I feel. It bothers me that my dad isn't here with me, especially now. I would like to think that when you die you go to Heaven and you "look down" on the ones you love, but who really knows.

I have been taking the anti-nausea meds as directed by my oncologist and the chemo nurses, since they were not happy with me at my first chemotherapy when I told them I really hadn't been following the medication schedule as directed. I'm still not taking the suppository, but now when I wake up in the middle of the night sick to my stomach, I take another anti-nausea pill instead of grinning and bearing the sickness, like I was doing. However, there is a downside to that too. Taking those anti-nausea meds means constipation! Ugh! Let's just say I haven't "dropped the kids off at the pool" in two days! I have been trying to eat prunes and have been putting bran in everything I eat. I feel like I'm an 80-year-old. I will say though, taking these meds properly I do feel much better. My mom took me back to the Cancer Center the day after chemotherapy to get the booster shot again but also get some fluids. I will be going back in a couple of days to get more fluids as well. I just can't seem to drink enough. I have noticed from the first treatment that having the extra fluids is really helping. The booster shot has some side effects. I was told I would feel achy, or have flu-like symptoms. I woke up this morning feeling very achy.

Since this second chemo, I'm either crying or I'm angry. I feel like I can't show these emotions to anyone, though. My mom has Olivia today and Alaina is with her dad. Landon is with his grandparents and my boyfriend had to work all day, so I am alone. Which is good, because I can cry or be mad all I want and no one is here to ask me what's wrong.

I got in the shower and was washing my hair, and every time I ran my fingers through it, my hair just kept falling out. I thought to myself, *this is the last time I will have to wash my hair for a long time*. I ran a comb through it and it just kept falling out. There is hair all over my pillow, all over the floor, it's just everywhere. I knew this was going to happen but it wasn't "real" for a long time. Now it's "real" and it's just another thing I have to face.

Chapter 17

November 5, 2012

GI Jane

"My hair just keeps falling out, you have to shave it for me." That's what I said to my boyfriend yesterday when my hair kept falling out. As I said before, whenever I put my fingers through my hair, at least five strands would come out. We had hair all over the pillows, the sheets, the floor, and mostly in my hands because I can't stand when my hair falls in my face, so I'm constantly pushing it back... I guess I don't have to worry about that anymore.

My boyfriend got out his buzzer, we talked for a few minutes about if I really wanted to buzz my remaining hair off. He thought it was a good idea since we were just going to have to clean up the floor all the time if I just let it fall out by itself. I went back and forth a few times - "Yes, let's do it," "No, I don't want to." "Ugh, okay, just do it." I knew this time was going to come but like everything else I've had to experience through this hell, until it's actually looking me in the face, it's just not real to me. I sat on the edge of the tub and my boyfriend started shaving my head. It's kinda funny to hear myself say that, my boyfriend shaved my head.

I held it together pretty well, seeing long hairs falling all around me with every shave he made. I wanted to cry but I didn't. When he was done, I got up, turned around and saw all my hair in the tub. Now, I've seen pictures of myself as an infant with "peach fuzz" but when you're a baby, you're cute no matter what. I looked in the mirror and I wanted to scream, cry, and just hit something hard. I didn't do any of that. I think as an adult woman, it's a big shock to see yourself with "peach fuzz." I looked at my boyfriend and said, "I don't want to see myself anymore, let's take down the mirrors." He said, "I think you look hot." Hot?! I know he was trying to lift my spirits, but come on, man! He said, "Hun, you have a pretty face and that didn't change because I shaved your head." I know my face hasn't changed but the way I look at myself has.

My mom came over to drop Livvy back home. I came around the corner with my "peach fuzz," to surprise her. She said, "Wow, you look really good." Mom... come on. My mom is the best, and no matter what I have on or what I look like, she still tells me I look good. She's a mom and her daughter has cancer, she has to say uplifting things, it's kind of in the handbook. But I knew she really did mean it.

My daughter Olivia just looked at me with a nervous laugh. "Livvy, what do you think?"

Still nervously laughing, she said, "You look weird." Well, yes... I do look weird.

"Are you afraid of me?" Livvy said no, that she wasn't afraid of me, but that I just looked different. Before my daughter Alaina came home, I was nervous that she wasn't going to want to come near me. Remember, this is the child that doesn't like anything "ugly" or "gross." I immediately thought she was going to think Mommy was ugly now that I didn't have hair. When Alaina came in, she looked at me like I had nine heads!

"Hi Lane! What do you think?" Alaina was very stand-offish and said, "You still look good."

I said, "Okay, who told you to say that to me?"

Alaina replied, "Daddy." I told her I really didn't want her to be afraid of me. She asked me if I would put a hat on. So I did, we tried on all my new hats and I showed her my new earrings I had bought a while ago for this very occasion. Alaina said, "I thought you weren't gonna have any hair at all, but you still have a little." I then told her that I would be completely bald soon enough.

I'm not looking forward to being "Mr. Clean" bald, I'm just getting used to my "GI Jane" look. When I plucked my eyebrows the other day, it was easier and didn't hurt at all. I really don't want to lose my eyebrows or my eyelashes, but I know that is the next thing I need to face, it's just not "real" yet.

Chapter 18

November 9, 2012

Physically Vs. Mentally

It's been a week since chemotherapy and right now I'm physically feeling great. Mentally is a different story. The chemo was easier on my body this time, despite the aches and pains from the booster shot. I wasn't as sick, I haven't had heart palpitations or headaches. The first time around I was feeling back to normal on the sixth day after chemo. This time it's taken seven days, and I feel recuperation time may be longer and longer each time around.

I feel so bad for the people who have to be or want to be around me lately. Mentally, I'm not all here, I am really moody. I have always had a short fuse but now it's gotten shorter. Everything gets me upset lately. I have broken down crying two nights this week... only two I think that's pretty good. I just don't feel like myself anymore. I have said this so many times, but this whole situation doesn't seem real to me. I'm going to wake up tomorrow and this will all just be a bad dream, no more eating pizza rolls before bed.

I'm Still Here

This isn't a bad dream, is it? This is actually my life. I keep asking myself, what did I do that was so bad to deserve this? Murderers, rapists, child molesters, those are the people that should get cancer and have their lives turned upside down, not me! Not good people! I know, I know - life isn't fair.

I can't really say I'm getting used to my new look, it freaks me out a lot. I go by a mirror and look twice, and I still can't believe I'm bald. For now, I still have my eyebrows and eyelashes so that makes me feel a little "normal." I have to be honest, I'm a little embarrassed, which sounds weird because I'm basically saying I'm embarrassed of my own head. The same head I have had for 30 years, just hidden under a mop of hair. However, the mop of hair that I had made me feel much better about myself. Before this diagnosis, I was very vain (which I blame my dad for) - I never went anywhere without makeup, I was obsessed about my weight (another thing we can blame on Dad), I was just always conscious about my appearance, worrying about what someone would think about me if I wasn't dressed well or if I ate that or if my hair wasn't in place. I spent most of my life worried about what people thought about my appearance. So, since my diagnosis, I have decided I really don't care what other people think about me. I'm gonna be bald for a while, I'm gonna eat bowls of pasta and pizza rolls before I go to bed, my nails aren't going to be pretty, and I may have to wear ugly glasses until the chemotherapy is over, because it's drying out my eyes and irritating my contacts. Either you like me for me, or you don't. I'm not losing sleep over it though! There is so much more to life than what other people think about you.

Chapter 19

November 11, 2012

Walk in My Shoes

Five little tidbits about chemotherapy....

#1. Chemo is cumulative, meaning it has to build up in the body. Which was why the second week after the first chemo treatment, I was feeling great and eating anything and everything. This second week after the second chemo has been a bit worse, I tire easily and my stomach hasn't been up to par. I can only assume that the second week after the third chemo treatment is going to be even worse, which completely sucks because that's the week of Thanksgiving and I love to eat turkey with all the fixins! I really don't think you understand how much I love to eat.

#2. "Chemo brain" IS real. I have heard this from a few people who underwent chemo and now I'm beginning to notice it. It's like when you're pregnant and do something stupid, or just get forgetful, everyone laughs and says, "Oh, we will blame that on pregnancy brain." Well, I have found that chemo makes you forgetful as well. This is totally serious, people. I made pumpkin bread the other day, put it in the oven, did all the dirty dishes and went in the living room to watch television. An hour went by and I thought to myself, *huh, what's that smell?* DING! The bell went off in my head - oh shit, I forgot I made pumpkin bread! Luckily pumpkin bread takes an hour to bake so it survived.

#3. Chemo takes over your emotions. I'm telling ya, I can deal with the nausea, even the heart palpitations but the emotional roller coaster ride from hell is starting to break me down. So far for me, this has been all emotional. I'm getting used to the "golf ball" in my chest (port) but not having hair is really depressing. I know you think it's just hair, it will grow back, no big deal. Except this is really a big deal for me. I also have been second-guessing everything in my life - my relationship, my friendships, if I'm being a good mom, and what I really want in life. A lot of people have told me, after this is over, I'm going to know exactly what I want out of life and exactly who I want to keep in it... right now it's looking like a short list.

#4. I recently found out that it is a fact: younger women feel more nauseous than older women. That's very interesting to me, I would have thought the opposite. Again, I can do nauseous all day. In fact, most of my life I was nauseous. When I was only eight, I got very sick, I stopped eating, was very pale, and lost a bunch of weight. Of course, my mom brought me to all the doctors and they ran lots of tests. Come to find out, I had an "overdose" of "bad" bacteria in my intestines. It took a while to diagnose but when they did, it was an easy fix. A couple of years after that, I was getting sick again, back to the drawing board! This time the doctors said I had IBS (irritable bowel syndrome), which I do nothing to relieve. Personally, I think it's a nervous stomach but if they want to say IBS, who am I to disagree. Also, I've been pregnant three times, and was terribly nauseous with all three. Nausea is nothing compared to some of the other stuff happening to my body.

#5. Chemo is exhausting. Just going to the Cancer Center and getting pumped up with crazy cocktails, you really wouldn't think that would make you tired. I mean, I'm sitting in a recliner the whole time. For some reason it does. I always want to go to bed after. Also, doing little chores around the house wipes me out. I usually never nap during the day, I have too much to do. Lately though, when Landon goes down for his nap, I have to lie down, too.

Fun fact about Corey: for some strange reason, for the first three days after chemo, I feel the need to watch Tim Allen in Christmas movies.

I can recite *Christmas with the Kranks* and *The Santa Clause 3* word for word.

Let's talk about death. That's right, I said the "d" word. This is not me being negative, I just think all the cards should be on the table. Anyone who gets diagnosed with any type of cancer automatically thinks they are going to die. You can say no all you want but even the most positive people in the world would think about it at least once if they were diagnosed with cancer. Do I think I'm going to die of breast cancer? Most days... no. However, it is always in the back of my mind that I could die from this. I am not afraid to die, I am afraid of missing out on seeing my children grow up. When I was a little girl, I couldn't wait to grow up. I wanted to be married and have kids and live happily ever after, like all the princess stories promised me. Life isn't always happily ever after though, is it?

So, my teenage years were no fun, and my twenties were very rocky. When I turned 30 this year, I swore things were going to get better because I thought they really couldn't get any worse... boy, was I wrong! Never in a million years did I think I was going to have cancer, especially not in my thirties. This just makes me see my life in a whole new way. It also makes me want to accomplish things sooner than I would normally have. Someone told me (and I won't name names) that I want everything now now now, well... can you blame me?! I have an illness that could kill me, put yourself in my shoes and tell me you wouldn't want everything "now now now." I believe that when it's your "time to go," you go. There's no stopping it. So, if I'm meant to die of breast cancer in my thirties, I can't change that.

I was going to stop going out to the stores altogether because I was afraid I would catch a cold or get the flu. Truth is, if I'm meant to get a cold or something else that could affect my heath, it's going to happen. Could I try to prevent it? Yes, but I can't live in a bubble, can I? I told all my friends that if they wanted to see me they would need to get flu shots first, which I actually got some complaints about! So much for wanting to see your friend! It just makes me think, if I have to beg you to come visit me, or beg you to get a simple flu shot, then don't bother. My point is, I don't really know how long I have to live, no one does, sick or not. With that said, I'm going to live my life, I'm going to do things I want to do and see everything life has to offer me and if you want to be a part of it, great! If not, stop wasting your time and my time. I don't mean to sound cruel, but put my shoes on for a minute and see if you can walk in them.

Chapter 20

November 19,2012

Me and My Bald Head

It's been four days since my third chemo treatment. I'm feeling pretty good. I'm saying this with my fingers crossed, praying to God and knocking on wood, but I really haven't experienced any real bad days yet. I am much more tired than the first two treatments, but my stomach is holding up pretty well this time around... well, so far anyway. I am in pain, though, the day after the booster shot I feel like I'm 80 years old. Every joint in my body aches. I have also noticed that around the third day after chemo, I get very antsy. I want to crawl out of my skin, I can't stay still, nothing relaxes me. I'm kinda thinking it could be because of the steroids I'm given during chemotherapy? Either that or I've developed ADHD.

My mom went with me this time to my appointment. I was glad she came this time because what we didn't know before we got to my appointment was that we were going to hear some interesting news that I think she needed to hear for herself.

Before I get chemo, I see my oncologist and we go over how I've been feeling since the prior treatment. She also does a breast exam to see if the tumor has changed at all. My oncologist asked me what I thought about the lump, if I thought it had changed at all. My response was, "I want you to tell me what you think first." See, the night before my appointment, I was in the shower washing up, but I couldn't feel the lump this time. So, when the oncologist asked me what I thought, I didn't want to say anything because I didn't want to look crazy if she still felt the lump in full force.

Drum roll please... I'm not crazy! She couldn't feel the lump anymore, either! She even went back to her notes to double-check that she was feeling the right spot. I wanted to leap off the table and jump for joy but I didn't, I stayed calm. My oncologist then told us that sometimes after undergoing chemotherapy, the tumors get very soft and almost get to like a jelly substance. This is very good for me because it means less surgery in the long run... I hope.

I have tried to be more positive since my last chemo. Now I can actually see the light at the end of the tunnel, even though it flickers at times. Hearing the news about my tumors has really put me in good spirits. At least now I know I'm not going through hell for nothing. It's only been three treatments, but they're working!

Emotionally, I feel as though I'm coping better. I decided to "bic" my head. Those of you who aren't familiar with the term, it just means I took a razor and shaved the rest of the peach fuzz off my head. The patchy peach fuzz was really getting to me, I looked like an old man. The other day, when everyone was out of the house, I took the razor and I "bic'd" it. I can't explain the feeling I have about the way I look. I'm not happy about the fact that I have a shiny bald head, like my ex-husband, but I do feel a little better about it now that it's not patchy. With the patchy peach fuzz, I was embarrassed, but now I'm okay with it. I'm not going to go into a store without a hat or a scarf on my head, I'm not that bold yet, but hanging around the house with my bald head out has gotten easier, and if my neighbors happen to see me and my bald head, so be it. I'm cool with it.

Chapter 21

November 24, 2012

The Laundry List

I started journaling because I wanted everyone to hear my story, I want to be able to help people who are or will be in my position. I also want to educate the caretakers, family, and friends of breast cancer victims. I have gone through and explained each and every test I have had to take along on this rocky road I'm traveling. I have also been very blunt when it comes to my experience with chemotherapy. I have tried to explain how my emotions are up and down and all over the place and how I am physically feeling after chemo.

With that said, I think it's time to dive into the "meat" of this experience. Plain and simple... chemo SUCKS! I have said before, breast cancer hasn't physically hurt me, what is hurting me is the treatment to essentially kill the cancer. My sister Beth took me to get fluids the other day, and as we were talking to the nurse about how I have been feeling, Beth said to me, "This is what you should journal about." There is so much that goes into "how I'm feeling" before and after each chemo treatment that if I don't write it down, I end up forgetting and moving on to a bigger problem. So,

I've decided to write a list of all my ailments since I've started chemotherapy. This doesn't mean that you or someone you know will have the same issues as me. Everybody is different, I just want to inform you of what CAN happen.

One of my biggest problems (that I resolved with extra fluids): **Heart palpitations and headaches**. If you have never had a heart palpitation, you might freak out and think your heart was stopping. That's what I thought the first time it happened to me. Scared the %&#@ out of me! Funny thing is, my doctor never mentioned these palpitations, just explained that chemo has a long-term effect on your heart. I have a history of migraines, so when the doctor told me I would have a "small" chance of getting headaches, I knew I would definitely get them. However, like I said, this all ended once I started getting fluids pumped into me every week. Just goes to show... HYDRATION IS KEY!

Nausea... I was only getting nauseous when I wasn't taking the nausea meds correctly. It's not like it was back in the day when the minute you got chemo running through your veins you needed to vomit. I don't ever feel sick to my stomach anymore, because I'm taking the nausea meds as directed. Some people I have talked to can't take the nausea meds because of all of the additional side effects from them, so they find other ways to cope with nausea. Medical marijuana, acupuncture, massage, yoga or reiki are just a few I've heard that help work to fight against nausea.

Side effects from the nausea meds: **Constipation, blurry vision, and headaches**. Yes, it sucks! And I've said before I don't want to be constipated, but I had to weigh my options. I am constantly eating bran and prunes to fight off constipation and so far, I haven't had blurry vision. Headaches come and go, but as long as I hydrate, I am okay. I don't want to feel sick to my stomach all the time.

I have noticed by the third day after chemo that I am climbing the walls. I want to rip my skin off, I feel so **antsy**. I don't like this feeling, I don't know who would, but nothing I do makes it go away and people, I take Xanax! I recently found out that the steroid given to me while I'm getting chemo makes me antsy like this and also one of the nausea meds I take has a "climbing the wall" effect. This is not fun and I have yet to relieve it.

Tingling in the fingers and toes. This is no fun either. Since probably three weeks ago, I have noticed my fingers and toes get very cold and almost feel numb. My oncologist told me that this could happen. Once it gets to the point where I can't feel anything, then we have a problem but for now it is just another side effect.

Dry skin. You wouldn't think this would be such a big deal but it is. Not only are my fingers cold and numb but also cracking because they are drying out so much. Lotion, lotion, lotion!

I think I mentioned before that all I want to eat is pasta and potatoes or anything I can drench in red sauce. I haven't mentioned, though, that I can't put anything sweet into my stomach until at least eight days after chemo. If I do, my stomach curdles. I'm not just talking chocolate, I'm saying pure sugar, Kool-aid, lemonade, sweet breads, syrups, anything that has pure white sugar added to it, I can't touch it.

Metallic taste and mouth sores: I haven't experienced this yet, and hopefully never will. This is a classic side effect of chemo. The only thing I can say for not having this yet is maybe because I went to the dentist before I started chemo and got a cleaning. I also use Biotene mouthwash around the clock, Biotene toothpaste, and I floss regularly. I never did this before. I was lucky to get to the dentist once a year and I only brushed my teeth every morning, forget about flossing. Since I have had chemo I'm all over it! I don't want to get mouth sores or have that metallic taste.

Runny nose and teary eyes: Ugh! This drives me nuts! My nose is constantly running, it's like having a cold that just won't go away. Also, my eyes burn and tear all the time. I swear everyone thinks I'm crying when in actuality, my eyes are just watery.

Fatigue: I have three children. I have been tired ever since my oldest daughter was born eight years ago! I really thought I knew what it was like to be exhausted... boy, was I wrong! The other day, I was cleaning up nail polish off the rug because my daughter spilled it... oh yeah, life doesn't stop, people... I got up from the floor and felt so drained. Simple little things like changing Landon's crib sheet or sweeping up the floor gets me so winded and tired. It's not a yawning tired, either. This feels like I just ran a 5K. My heart races, I feel very clammy, and I get dizzy. It almost feels like I'm suffocating, this is by far the worst feeling ever, and it happens ALL the time. I sit down more now than I ever have, and I try to get a nap in when Landon goes down for his nap.

Joint aches and pains: The day after I have chemo, I get a Neulasta shot. This shot is to boost up my white blood cells. Apparently it attacks the bone marrow in my body, though. There is a laundry list of side effects from this little shot, but I have only experienced the joint aches and pains, which is enough! I wake up that next day sore and every joint in my body hurts, I don't want to move, but again... life doesn't stop just because I'm going through chemo.

Hair loss: Everyone knows this is a side effect from chemo, all of the hair on your body goes if you get a certain concoction of chemotherapy. I think the doctors know exactly which chemo will make your hair fall out so if they are telling you "it might fall out," I think they just want to spare your feelings.

So, put all those together, add in some heartburn and the everlasting upset stomach, and that's pretty much a normal day for me. That's just all the physical stuff, that's all the things I can bitch about. The mental stuff, the stuff I need to hold in, that's another story! If you are caring for someone who is undergoing chemotherapy or just trying to be a friend to them, all I can say to you is just have patience. This is a very emotional road trip and if you're on it, be prepared for some pretty abrupt turns.

I am not the person who asks for help or who wants people to know I need help. I'm also not the person who wants to show she's not feeling well. I'm actually embarrassed to get sick in front of people. Since going through this, I do need help. I am very fortunate to have my family and friends to help me along this journey. They drive me crazy sometimes, and sometimes I just want to be alone, and sometimes I just want to go somewhere with lots of people and not care about getting germs, or go to a doctor's appointment by myself. This is not forever and I know that. This experience has changed the way I see everything in my life, and though I never want to walk this road again, I have to believe it happened for a reason.

Chapter 22

November 28, 2012

Counting My Chickens

Thanksgiving is my very favorite holiday. We don't do anything, just stay home all day in our pajamas, watch Christmas movies and the parade, cook dinner, and eat all day long. I love Thanksgiving!

Well... Thanksgiving came and went. It was quiet. I got to watch the Macy's Day Parade. I ended up cooking for the five of us. I never really thought cooking was such a big deal because I enjoy cooking. However, when you're not as healthy as you used to be, it becomes a big deal. I cooked everything from the 21-pound turkey down to the deviled eggs, with my boyfriend's help cleaning out the turkey guts... yuck. I also made pie and a cake. It took hours to make everything and about 15 minutes to eat it all. Well... I wore myself out. The next day I was so tired and winded, I had that suffocating feeling again, I felt awful. My mom convinced me to call the Cancer Center and when I did they asked me to come in for blood work. My lab results showed that my red blood count had dropped from 14 to 11. If it had gone down to a 9, I would have had to receive a blood transfusion. Also, my potassium went down as well. I was feeling really crappy. They gave me some more fluids and let me go home. By Sunday, I was much better.

My last AC chemo is in a couple of days, I'm very excited about this! I call it AC but it really has a big long name I can't pronounce. AC is very hard on the body. I will have had four ACs in total. I still have twelve more Taxol chemo treatments, but I've heard the Taxol twelve won't be as bad. I have had chemo three times, so I know what to expect for this last one, but for some reason I'm very nervous about this last AC. I know two days after the chemo treatment, I will feel crappy and I will want to sleep all day. After that I will be climbing-the-walls antsy. This time I'm going to take Xanax throughout the day to see if it will relieve the antsy feeling. A few days after that, I will feel better but still not good. That next week is what gets me nervous. I know I'm counting my chickens, but really, this is the stuff I worry about... the stuff I can't control. I was so totally wiped out after the last chemo that I felt like I was suffocating. I don't want to feel that way again. Since chemotherapy is cumulative, I'm worried that I won't be able to do much of anything at all.

I saw my surgeon today. She did a breast exam and was pleased to see how good the chemo is working. My biggest tumor was 4-5 cm. That's like the size of a silver dollar, which is a little hard for me to process since if you've seen me in person you know I'm very small-chested, so I don't know where I'm hiding this tumor. The surgeon couldn't feel it this time. She did feel my lymph node but she said it was much smaller than when I first came in to see her. This is good news but... yes, there is always a BUT... My problem is I can hear all this good news about how the chemo is working and I can soak it all in, but I still want the big question answered. Am I going to survive this?! No one will answer that question and until they do, I'm going to keep thinking the worst. You know that expression, hope for the best but prepare for the worst? Yes, that's totally me. I can smile and be upbeat and positive to everyone I see, but really, I'm thinking the absolute worst.

Chapter 23

December 2, 2012

See Ya, AC!

I'm so happy!!! I completed the AC chemo treatments!! I am very excited to say this; however, this has been by far the worst I have felt since starting chemo. One of my friends came over to watch Landon the day after I had chemo so I could rest, then that night I went for my last booster shot and got some fluids, too. The next morning, my boyfriend took Landon to work with him, so I would be able to rest. I remember looking at the clock before they left, it was 7:30. I kissed them goodbye and fell back asleep. I woke up about two hours later, but I couldn't move. My joints were all kinked up. Luckily, my boyfriend put my cell phone next to me, in the bed, before he left. I remember being barely able to hold the cell phone, I was in so much pain. I called my mom to come over and help me. Like I have said before, I don't like to ask for help, but this time I really needed it.

Mom came over, (luckily, she has a key to get in), and helped me get out of bed, she made me breakfast, and did some cleaning around the house At one point I heard her crying while she was washing my dishes. I can't imagine how my mom feels, seeing her daughter, her baby, fighting for her life. I had a slight meltdown, and told my mom I didn't want to do any more treatments, that I was all done with this shit. I hate seeing my mom cry, and knowing that I'm the reason that she's sad makes me feel awful.

I know I can't just stop the treatments but, at that moment, I was ready to be done. I was pretty much in bed that whole day. I slept on and off. Every time I woke up I was in pain, this being because of the booster shot I get after the AC treatments. Since this was my last AC, this was also my last booster shot. Thank goodness! Hopefully, I won't feel like I'm 80 years old anymore.

I've been through two months of treatments, and I can't even believe how fast it has gone by. I have felt so awful at times. I have seen myself get weak and physically change (*i.e.*, the bald head). I have been on the bathroom floor crying my eyes out, not wanting to live at times. I have felt so completely miserable and have been upset with everyone around me. This was a road I wanted to travel alone. I didn't want the people that I love seeing me this way. I didn't want to be a burden on anyone. I realize now that no one going through this hell should ever be alone in it. I know who loves me and who my friends are, that they need to see me just as much as I need to see them. I know I'm not a burden to those who want to help me and who care about me. Unfortunately, I had to be put through hell to see it.

Chapter 24

December 8, 2012

Worry Wart

I met with both my surgeon and oncologist last week, at different times. My surgeon didn't do a breast exam this time because she already got word from my oncologist that my tumors could not be felt anymore. I guess as a surgeon she has to trust what her colleague says. As the patient, I'm thinking, *come on, lady, don't you want to make sure yourself?* The surgeon did check my lymph nodes though, which she could still feel but said were much smaller. At this moment, I know for sure that there is only one lymph node that is cancerous, because that's what they can feel. Once they open me up for surgery, they could find others. Now, my question is, four weeks ago my oncologist did a breast exam and couldn't feel the tumors anymore. So does that mean it couldn't have grown back in those next few weeks? I still think both of them should have done a breast exam. I know this is just me being worried, when I should just be grateful that everything is shrinking and the chemo is actually working to kill the cancer.

These last few days since my last AC have really been hard on me. I can't say it enough, I am just worn out. Every little move I make just makes me tired. After the third chemo treatment, it took eight days for me to feel better. Right now I'm on day eight, so I'm hoping to feel back to normal very soon.

I start Taxol, the next chemo treatment, on the 13th. Everyone, nurses, my doctor, and breast cancer survivors have told me that Taxol will be so much better on my body then the AC was. I really hope so because I never want to feel like this again. My oncologist explained that I will have to take five steroids the night before chemo and the morning of chemo. This worries me a little, but what doesn't worry me these days?! Apparently, some people can have an allergic reaction to Taxol (a very small percentage). So, they will load me up with steroids and Benadryl just to help reduce the risk of an allergy. The nurse also told me that during the treatment she will be checking on me every 15 minutes to make sure I'm not having a reaction. Do they really need to tell me this? Don't they know who I am?! I'm a constant worry wart! I have now been driving myself crazy, thinking that I won't be able to have this treatment because I'll be allergic to it, and because of that I will die. THE END. I know what you're saying - does it always have to come down to death? How can a person in my position not think about dying, though?!

Let's list the facts, shall we?

I have breast cancer.

It is aggressive.

My tumors could not be felt after my second chemo treatment.

I have accomplished four AC treatments.

I have 12 Taxol treatments to go.

I need surgery and radiation.

Not a very positive list; however, I see this as, although only having been through two treatments, we know it's working and working well. That gives me lots of hope. I just need it to keep working for another three to four months. After that, surgery, and then I can breathe again... I hope.

I'm not going to die of breast cancer. I'm not. I keep saying that. Over and over and over again, one day really soon I'm going to believe it.

Chapter 25

December 17, 2012

Strong

My mom took me to my first Taxol treatment. Before the treatment, I met with my oncologist. She examined my lymph node again to see if there was any change from my last AC treatment two weeks ago. The oncologist said she could still feel it but that it was getting smaller and narrower. Good news!

As you all know, I was very nervous about starting the next phase of chemo. The night before my treatment I had to take five steroids. I also had to take five steroids the morning of treatment. After seeing my oncologist, (like I usually do before I receive the poison, oops I mean chemo), I went into a "pod" to get my treatment. My nurse also gave me more steroids, Benadryl, Zyrtec and, because I was feeling weird after all of that medicine, she gave me a sedative to try to calm my nerves. Taxol can have an allergic reaction, which is why they pumped me full of meds before giving me the Taxol. As you can imagine after getting all those drugs intravenously, I was pretty sleepy. I dozed in and out the whole time. Eleven more treatments to go!

The next morning, I woke up feeling okay, I didn't need any nausea meds and I was eating and drinking like I normally would. I did have to call the Cancer Center because I was feeling pressure in my chest and my face was very flushed. They told me to come in and be seen, just to make sure nothing was really wrong. My mom came over to watch Landon and get the girls off the bus so I could go to the Cancer Center. I was there for three hours! I had an EKG, a chest X-ray, and blood work. I was also seen by a PA and my oncologist. Everything turned out fine and I was told I was probably feeling the pressure and the flushed face because of all the steroids I was on.

I have written little bits and pieces about things that have happened to me in my short 30 years on earth and some things I just can't talk about. Things that no one should have to see or go through. Now, don't get me wrong, I know there are a lot of people worse off than me, but someone had to be Corey. I'm glad I have these experiences under my belt; they've made me the person I am today. If you asked me 10 years ago to name good qualities about myself, strong would not have made the list. I never thought of myself as being strong-minded, although 10 years ago nothing bad had happened to me, I didn't have kids, I had no worries in the world... life was good. I know that life can change in a matter of minutes, suddenly there are worries and hardships and sadness. I am a strong person because I have been through a lot of crap and refuse to take the easy way out, which trust me I've contemplated many times. So, when I was diagnosed with cancer, everyone was telling me to be strong. I never knew what that meant until now. For me being strong means to not give up. It means I will put on make-up every day and try to look my best even though inside I feel awful, but I will do this just so the people I love will think, okay, she looks good so she must be feeling good. I will play games and color with my kids just so they won't think Mommy is sick. I will push myself to do the laundry and the dishes, and to make dinner because that's how I know how to be strong.

There are so many twists and turns in life. Since starting chemo, I notice now that when I get very upset I get weak, tired, my heart goes crazy and I shake. Taking care of my kids has been very hard for me, too. If you're going through chemo, make sure you have a full-time nanny, cook, or maid. This is by far the hardest thing I have ever done.

Chapter 26

December 24, 2012

Diarrhea Dilemma

Remember how I had said everyone I talked to had told me that Taxol was going to be way better on my body? I'm not so sure I believe them. I had another rough week. After the first Taxol treatment, my stomach was a mess, and the very next day I started having diarrhea. You remember how worried I was about being constipated, right? Let me tell you, I don't know what's worse, having diarrhea or being constipated. I thought maybe the diarrhea was because I have IBS (irritable bowel syndrome) and one of the laundry list of side effects from Taxol is diarrhea so I just figured it was because of the combination of the two.

Chemo lasts in your system only about three days, so I just thought after the three days were up I would be better again. After those three days came and went, I was still having diarrhea. I called the Cancer Center to see what I could do. They told me they wanted me to come in and be seen and that I should take Imodium. If you don't know what Imodium is, then you've never experience horrible diarrhea, and if that's the case I envy you. Imodium is like air to those of us that have experienced the runs. It's necessary and works like magic!

I must have looked like death when I went into the center that day because the secretary, the nurses, and the PA that I saw all told me I didn't look so hot. They basically told me I needed fluids and that I should take the Imodium. Okay, easy enough, hook me up. The next day came along and I was still feeling awful and still crapping up a storm, so off to the Cancer Center I went. I met with yet another PA who said because I was still having this problem I was going to need stool samples and a CT scan.

"Wait a minute... did you say stool samples?!" That's exactly what I said to the PA, she then said, "Yes, if you can go here that would be great and we could get things moving along." WHAT?! I said very bluntly, "I don't poop in public," which she got a laugh at but I was totally serious, there was no way I was giving them "samples" right then and there. The PA also told me that since I was having such a problem with my stomach that they didn't want me to get chemotherapy the next day when I was scheduled for it. Okay, so one part of me was like, hell yeah, I don't have to have chemo this week, but the other part of me said, I want to get this over and done with, I don't want to miss out on a treatment. They also said I wouldn't be able to get chemo because they wanted a CT scan first just to make sure the Taxol wasn't giving me colitis. I went home after getting more fluids and told my family that I wasn't getting chemo the next day but that I still needed to go to the hospital to get the Herceptin (which is the other part of my treatment for the Her2 gene) and more fluids. I also had an echocardiogram that same morning. Since I wasn't getting chemo, I could drive myself.

I got up early that morning, and Mom came over to watch Landon for me. I got to the hospital and had to wait 40 minutes until my echocardiogram. Let me explain about the echo. The chemo that I'm receiving can damage the heart, so I have to get echos every couple of months just to make sure it's not putting a strain on my heart. My echo was also done by a man, which I was a little upset about. He was very nice and professional but I'm just not comfortable with a strange man putting his hands on my bare chest through a little hospital gown. After my echo, I had about an hour and half until my appointment with my oncologist. I ended up leaving the hospital to bring my boyfriend some breakfast while he was at work. Yes, I am an awesome girlfriend. When I got back to the Cancer Center I met with my oncologist. She explained to me that she was very concerned about me because my vitals showed that my blood pressure had gone up, my heart rate had gone into the 120s and I had lost six pounds. She also felt my stomach to see if she could feel anything abnormal to see if we really needed the CT scan. She felt nothing. My oncologist then said, "I think you're having diarrhea because of your IBS and the Taxol/Herceptin mix." I'm pretty sure I said that from the beginning but who am I?! That being said, there was no reason why I couldn't have the chemotherapy. Well, wait a second... firstly, I didn't bring anyone to drive me home. Secondly, I hadn't taken the steroids the night before because they assured me I wasn't getting the chemo. Now I was nervous. Again, I really don't want to miss out on any treatment, but I wasn't able to prepare myself for this one.

I pretty much slept the whole time during my chemo treatment. The Benadryl knocked me out. I stayed there longer than usual and I ended up driving myself home. I was okay, but I don't think I want to chance it again because I had a hard time keeping my eyes open driving home. I went back to the Cancer Center the next day to get fluids and to check my vitals. My oncologist wants me to go to the Cancer Center every day now, I guess it's a big deal that I lost weight and that I'm really not drinking. I still have been having diarrhea so they definitely wanted the stool samples, which I did do but in the privacy of my own bathroom.

Since starting the Taxol, I do have more energy and I'm not in pain since I don't need the booster shot anymore. However, the diarrhea issue is no good. There is no way I can keep having diarrhea for the next two months. Yesterday and today I have been eating yogurt with bananas before every meal and I have also been taking Xanax a couple of times a day. The Xanax seems to calm my stomach down and I haven't had the diarrhea issue today at all.

Christmas is in two days! I'm excited about it for the first time in a few years. Since my dad died, I just haven't been into the holidays. My dad died when I was 27, and we were very close. He loved Christmas, he would play Christmas music all year round. One year we actually had "Christmas in June." I understand now that it's okay to be sad about my dad, but it's not okay to be miserable because he's gone. Life goes on. If this breast cancer has taught me anything, it's that from now on I'm going to enjoy my life, my kids, my family, and friends because life is too short. I just keep thinking that by this time next year, all of this cancer crap will be behind me, not gone forever because breast cancer is a part of me now. Something I will never forget and always worry about returning.

Chapter 27

December 30, 2012

Quitting is Not an Option

I only have three words to say right now... I hate Taxol! I have had three Taxol treatments so far, and remember, I have 12 in total to complete. I think it's moving along pretty fast but certainly not fast enough. My poor intestines!

I was very happy on Christmas Eve when I could eat everything I wanted. Of course, I had to take an Imodium that morning and half of a Xanax every four hours to calm down my stomach, but it actually worked pretty well. I've been doing the every-four-hour Xanax regimen ever since and it seems to be working. Since being on this Godawful Taxol I do have much more energy than I did on the AC. That is the ONLY plus, however.

The other day, when I was getting fluids, I overheard an older woman talking to the nurse about how she was looking forward to Taxol because the AC was really hard on her. The nurse then replied, "Oh yes, Taxol will be so much better on your body." I wanted to yell across the room, "Yeah, that's what you told me too, but Taxol sucks!" Of course, I didn't say that. Everyone is different, so maybe this woman will feel like a million bucks on Taxol... I just don't. Which I blame on my stomach, if I didn't have stomach issues to begin with maybe I would breeze through Taxol.

As I was driving in the car today, I was thinking about people in the world who have to go through chemo. Does anyone breeze through chemo? I know some people handle it better than others, but is there anyone who's been through chemo and can actually say it wasn't that bad. Personally, I think I'm handling it pretty well, but in that same statement I can also say that it IS that bad.

I was ready to quit this whole chemo/cancer shit almost two weeks ago, I just couldn't take it anymore. I went in and talked to my oncologist about stopping the treatments. This isn't the most convenient time in my life to get sick. Ten years ago, now that would have been a better time for me but you don't get to pick when awful things happen to you. My oncologist didn't like my idea of stopping the chemo. She and two PAs all agreed that it wasn't a good idea at all, that I wouldn't be stopping the chemotherapy. Well, I don't like to be told what to do and usually I would do the opposite just because I don't like to be told what to do, but this time I know there is really no other way. If I stop treatments and pretend that I don't have cancer, I will die. My kids are eight, six, and fifteen months old, and I will be damned if my kids call someone else Mommy because I was selfish and quit my treatment. For once in my life, quitting is not an option for me.

Chapter 28

January 5, 2013

I'm Still Here

I can pretty much count the lashes on my eyelids. I knew this day was coming but I was hoping I would beat the odds and I wouldn't lose them. My eyebrows are still going strong so I'm happy about that. While I was putting makeup on this morning, my Olivia said, "Mommy, you really ARE losing your eyelashes." Ugh... Fake eyelashes here I come! I figure if Snookie can do it, so can I.

My fourth Taxol treatment went okay. I saw my oncologist first and we talked about what had been happening since my third treatment. I explained that I wasn't having the horrible diarrhea anymore but that I was still taking Imodium and Xanax. I have had some chest pressure which no one can really explain. It happens around the third day after chemo. I know it's not anxiety, because most of the time when I experience this pressure I'm just lying in bed watching television. I have had echocardiograms and chest CT scans, and everything checks out fine. The last time I felt that chest pressure, my arm and hand went numb at the same time. I immediately thought I was having a heart attack. Of course, I didn't say anything, I just rolled over and went to sleep. Here's the thing - when I feel like something is wrong with me, like the chest pressure or the numbness, instead of maybe telling someone about it or trying to fix it, I just go to sleep. I know, probably not the smartest move on my part but I'm still here.

The numbness in my fingers and toes is a common side effect from the Taxol. I feel it on and off but it's not something I'm too concerned about at this point.

My oncologist also told me that my blood count went down low. I'm not sure what a normal blood count is supposed to be, but mine is now at a 1000. My oncologist explained that I am now in danger of contracting a virus or getting an infection so I need to stay away from anyone who could be sick, and I should stay out of the stores. I wasn't too happy with this, because (1) I'm so tired of being in this house with a crying baby 24/7!! Don't get me wrong, I love my son but I'm going stir-crazy! (2) My oncologist also explained that if my count goes down again before my next treatment, I won't be able to receive the chemo until it goes back up. Here we go again! I can't explain to you how much I don't want to miss a treatment. Also, there's nothing I can do to bring up my blood count. I thought maybe I would load myself up with vitamin C and eat a lot of green leafy veggies and presto! My blood count would go up again. Nope!

My oncologist explained that there is nothing I can do to bring my blood count up. "It's your bone marrow and it has to heal itself." This just doesn't make sense to me. If I keep getting chemo every week, how are my counts ever going to go up? I talked to Miss Mandy and she told me that when she went through Taxol, her counts went so low that she missed two treatments. I also talked to another survivor who told me she missed one of her treatments because her blood count went down too low as well. Does anyone complete all these Taxol treatments?! I feel like I'm getting set up to fail here.

I guess 2013 isn't going to be my year. I still have two months of chemo, surgery in April, and then at least eight weeks of radiation. I'm looking forward to 2014, when this is all over and done with. If I didn't have cancer, my life would be different right now. I would be working, and doing things that I want to do, instead of hanging out at the Cancer Center twice a week! I want to believe this happened to me for a reason. Maybe this happened to me so I could tell my story.

Chapter 29

January 12, 2013

I Just Want to Look Normal!

Putting on eyelashes wasn't as bad as I thought it would be. They did peel off throughout the day, so I had to keep applying glue to them. I figure I'm not going to wear them every day, just the days I want to look NORMAL! I still have my eyebrows but now I have to pencil them in, because they are falling out, too. I had said over and over again that I wasn't going to get a wig, who am I trying to fool? Everyone knows I have cancer and am going through chemo, which is why I'm bald. The thing is, now that my lashes are going and my eyebrows are fading away, I'm starting to look like an alien. I guess all I can say is, I decided to get a wig to make me feel better about myself. I kinda like it, it takes my mind off the fact that I really don't have any hair at all.

I put my wig on before my boyfriend came home. I thought I would surprise him with my dazzling new look. He looked at me and said, "You look better without the wig." I should have taken that as a compliment, but I didn't, I thought I looked amazing in that wig and I wanted him to think I looked amazing, too. My daughters kinda chuckled when they saw me in the wig, so that's it, I'm never wearing this thing again, just call me Mr. Clean.

When I was little, I used to watch *The Fresh Prince of Bel Air*... a young Will Smith, still with me? One episode had Will Smith going to the prom with some pretty girl. I'm not sure about all the details, it was a long time ago, but something happened and they ended up locked in the maintenance room. The pretty prom date got mad, drama, drama, drama, and she pulled out her hair extensions, peeled off her eyelashes and snapped off her "press-on" nails, which led Will Smith to look at her like she was a totally different person. It's weird that I remember this one episode but my point is, I can relate to that girl. I understand the phrase "put my face on" much better now. At the end of my night, I go into the bathroom as a pretty-faced woman. While in the bathroom, I peel off my eyelashes, take my contacts out, take off my hat. Get out the makeup remover and remove my drawn-on eyebrows and the rest of my makeup. I come out of the bathroom looking like a completely different person... bald head, ugly glasses, pale skin with dark circles under my eyes. It's a wonder my family still recognizes me!

The fifth chemo went well, and my blood count went up to 1800, which was good because it allowed me to get chemo this week. A normal count is around 7000... 7000! I won't be back to normal for a long time but at least it's up again.

I ended up seeing my surgeon the day I had chemo. I have said this before, I never feel great after talking to my surgeon. She did say that she could not feel anything anywhere, which is really good! If she had stopped talking right there I would have left as a happy girl. Nope, she kept talking and getting me worried. She asked me what I want to do about surgery, that because I didn't test positive for the BRACA gene, I wouldn't have to get a mastectomy but because I could live another 50 years, there is a greater chance of a recurrence. This does not make me feel good. She went on and on but honestly, I was so doped up on the Benedryl they had given me for chemo, that at one point I just wanted to say to her, "Please stop talking because I'm really not hearing you." I didn't say that, I just kept nodding my head. I told her I was going to do what she thought was best for me. At this point, she thinks she can save the breast, just get the tumors out and take the two sections of the lymph nodes out.

I don't know how I feel about this. I don't ever want to go through this again, so having a mastectomy will ensure the cancer won't come back.

However, do I want a mastectomy? Do I want to go through reconstructive surgery? I just don't know yet. I still have some time to think about it, my surgery is booked for April 2, three months away, which everyone keeps telling me is a long way off. I started chemo in the beginning of October. October, November, and December flew by for me. I can only expect that these next three months will go by just as quick.

Chapter 30

January 19, 2013

Chemo Pro

I never had any awful thoughts about my tumors. I have talked to many survivors and most of them had surgery first. They hated the thought that the tumor was inside their body, they just wanted it out. I still don't feel that way. I have two tumors that are pretty big. When I felt the tumor for the first time, which back then seemed only to be this little lump that I thought could only be a cyst, I was panicked and upset about it but never had the thought that whatever it was, it needed to get out of me right away. I'm the type of person who thinks, if it's not broken don't fix it. My tumors never hurt me, I wasn't in any pain, so as long as you don't cause me pain, you can stay.

I was sitting in the Cancer Center the other day with three other cancer patients. One other woman was going through treatment but the other two were just starting. I felt like a pro, a chemotherapy pro!

"Is it true...?"

"No."

"Do you really...?"

"Yes." I was glad that I could answer their questions, but then I sat back and thought, *is this really happening?* I'm answering questions about chemotherapy, something only four months ago I knew nothing about. This is still so surreal to me. What were you thinking about when you were 30? I'm sure one of your thoughts wasn't to beat breast cancer.

The sixth chemo went well. Beth took me this time. We watched one of my very favorite movies, *Just Go With It*. Laughter is the best medicine, right? So why not play funny movies around the clock during chemotherapy? I really don't like watching the news when I'm there, it's depressing to know the world is falling to shit, especially when you're getting pumped up with poison.

I can drive myself to chemo and to get fluids now, but it is nice to have someone with me, especially during chemo because it's longer. It gives me a chance to catch up with the person who's with me and I get one-on-one time with them, no chaos with the kids. Beth is one of my favorite people, not just because she's my sister. I asked her once if she thought we would be friends if we weren't related, and she said no. I'm not offended, I think it's funny. We are ten years apart in age, but we do have similar interests, even though I question her humor. I think we would be friends. She helped my mom out a lot with caring for me when I was young; hell, she still does a lot for me even at 30. I don't hug her enough. In my will, if something were to happen to me and my ex-husband together (which would be really weird now that we are divorced), our daughters will go to Beth. Same thing if anything happened to me and my boyfriend together, our son Landon would go to Beth. I picked Beth because she does so much for my kids, she knows them almost as well as I do, and I think she is the closest to me. I don't mean close like we hang out all the time, because since I had kids we really don't hang out anymore. I mean close as in to my personality. I know she loves them, and she would keep them in line and raise them like I would want. I really don't think anything would ever happen to me and one of my baby daddies at the same time, however... I'm 30 years old with breast cancer, and no family history of it. I guess anything is possible.

I have six more chemo treatments! I can finally see the light at the end of the tunnel and this time it's not just flickering. I know I still have a long road ahead of me but knowing that I'm half-way through the hard part just keeps me pushing forward.

Talking to my oncologist left me feeling a little better about surgery and I think I know what I'm going to do now. I told her I never want to go through chemotherapy again. She then told me that if I were to get a lumpectomy now and the breast cancer came back in the future, it would be an automatic mastectomy, no more chemo. Like I said, I'm fine with a mastectomy, but I've heard having reconstructive surgery is painful and it takes over a year to complete and recuperate. After I complete chemo, surgery, radiation, and Herceptin, I will have lost a year of my life to cancer. I really don't want to lose another year to reconstructive surgery. Lumpectomy here I come!

Chapter 31

January 26, 2013

Preparing for Cancer?

After I had my son, I was having a lot of problems. Two months after he was born, I thought my appendix was going to burst. I had such bad pain on my right side. My primary care doctor sent me to get a CAT scan to see if anything was happening. The scan was fine, probably just gas. A couple of weeks later, my PCP sent me for an ultrasound of my thyroid because my blood levels weren't where they should have been. Of course, the ultrasound found something and I had to have a biopsy of my thyroid. That was awful! However, it came back negative. A month after that, I was doing the laundry and all of a sudden I went blind, then I started to see fuzzy and in a circle pattern. I went to the eye doctor immediately but everything checked out okay, probably just migraines. A few weeks after that, I was lying in bed and I started getting shooting pains in my head and my heart was going crazy. I called an ambulance because I thought I was dying. They took me to the hospital, where I had another CAT scan and they gave me some meds. They said everything was okay, but since the eye episode, they thought I was definitely suffering from migraines. A month after that, I fell twice and hit my head both times. Landon was only a few months old when all of this was happening to me. He was waking up every couple of hours around the clock, therefore I wasn't sleeping. I started feeling weird, and the only way I could explain it was like this: I told every doctor I saw (and there was a few) that I felt like I was drunk, except I could walk a straight line, drive, and do everything like normal. I thought it might be vertigo, but the room was never spinning. It was such an awful feeling, it wasn't like the nice feeling you get when you get tipsy. This was a horrible feeling that I hope I never have to feel again. I was going crazy. I started looking up my symptoms online. (Never Google your symptoms.) I saw a neurologist, because I thought I might have MS. She told me, "I'm almost sure you don't have MS. MS symptoms come on fast, like you would suddenly go blind or be unable to control your bladder." I have said before, your mind is a powerful thing and can screw with you. I must have been dwelling on what the neuro doc said, because two days after I saw her, I went blind in my left eye. It only lasted about three minutes but it scared the shit out of me. I went back to her and she sent me for an MRI to make sure it wasn't MS. Turned out it wasn't, but I was still having that weird drunk feeling. And I was so upset because no one could help me. In a matter of four months, I saw two eye doctors, my PCP five times, a neurologist twice, a thyroid doctor and an ENT. I had an MRI, two CAT scans, a truckload of blood work, and a biopsy. (I told you, I'm not new when it comes to doctors and tests.) Every doctor I saw said I was a normal, healthy 30-year-old, which just frustrated me more because I knew something was wrong. I'm very glad to say that after those four months, that drunk feeling went away. I think back now and I really should have been smarter. I fell and hit my head twice before that feeling started happening. I probably had a concussion and didn't realize it. Since Landon was waking me up every couple of hours, that threw my sleep schedule off and I couldn't rest. It makes sense to me now but back then I seriously thought I was dying.

I can remember telling my mom that I really believed something was wrong with me and that I thought I was dying. I can also remember texting Beth something about how I wanted her to have a good life and be happy. In turn she texted back, "OMG Corey, you're not dying!" So that winter came and left and so did all my symptoms. Last summer was looking up and I was starting to feel better, and then the other shoe dropped. Isn't it ironic? Last winter I seriously thought I was dying. This winter, I could actually be dying. Again, I'm not being negative, I'm just wondering if everything I was feeling last year was actually my body preparing for this... preparing for cancer.

Seven Taxol treatments down, five more to go! At the last minute, Beth ended up taking me to chemo. We had to wait a while just to get the chemo started. In the meantime, my "breast navigator" came in and talked to us. I love this woman, she comes with me to every test I have, every doctor's appointment, and I see her at almost every chemo. She went into more detail about my surgery. I asked if I was going to have to stay overnight after my lumpectomy. She said that because my surgeon has to take my lymph nodes out, and put in a drain, I will probably be staying the night, which sucks, I love my bed too much. Beth and I just looked at each other with sheer disgust when talk about a drain came up. EWWW. That was something that never crossed my mind. I just think about it and get grossed out, but at least it's only going to be in for a week or so.

Beth had bought me hair and nail collagen pills, so we asked my breast navigator if I could start taking them now or wait until chemo was over. She explained that because my liver is working so hard with this chemo, that I can't start taking those pills now. I also can't take any extra stuff like vitamin C or Theraflu, Airborne, nothing except for a multi vitamin. It would just cause too much strain on my liver. Also remember, I don't drink much which is why I get fluids twice a week through the port in my chest. I would assume the fluids help to flush out the chemo and meds that are going through my body, which helps my liver to function properly. Can you imagine if I didn't do that? My liver and my kidneys would be shot!

My daughter Olivia's teacher emailed me today. He voiced his concern that Livvy is getting very frustrated with her work, and when he took her out in the hall to cool down, she broke into tears. Apparently, Livvy told her teacher that she's very worried about me, and she's afraid I'm going to die. Her teacher said he thinks Olivia would benefit from seeing the school counselor. I know Livvy is worried about me, but knowing it's affecting her in school breaks my heart. I feel like I'm bringing my kids down. I have never told them I think I'm going to die or that I'm worried I am dying. I always tell them, Mommy will get better and be fine. I talked to Livvy about this after her teacher emailed me. She started to cry and talked to me a little bit. She just found out that the mom of one of Alaina's classmates died of cancer this week. Olivia is worried that I'm next.

I've said it many times, I don't think I'm going to die of breast cancer. This has interfered with every part of my life now. It just raises so many questions in my head. I think I got breast cancer for a couple of reasons: (1) I needed a wake-up call. Corey, if you take your life for granted, your life will be taken from you. I did take life for granted, I would get upset and angry over the stupidest little things. I'm learning to chill out a bit. I made a bucket list (if you haven't seen the movie, it's really worth watching), not because I think I'm going to die, but because I'm going to live and I want to do everything and see everything life has to offer. And (2), it's my time to help others in need. I believe I had to experience breast cancer and its treatment in order to really help others who have it. What doesn't kill us makes us stronger. Okay, I'm strong enough, lay off me for a little while!

Chapter 32

February 2, 2013

The Awkward Conversation

When I first started this journal, I knew I wanted to be as blunt and as real as possible through my cancer experience. I've been holding off on this conversation but recent issues that have been causing me trouble have brought me to this point, and I'm ready to dish.

The 1980s band Salt-N-Pepa said it straight out... Let's talk about sex. And now everyone in my family that is reading this book just put it down. I will admit, it's an awkward conversation to have at any age. However, the very first day I met with my oncologist, she told me I wasn't to get pregnant while going through chemo or while I am on Tamoxifen for the next five years. I am estrogen-positive so I can't take birth control anymore, so she suggested we take other precautions. Then she proceeded to ask, "Do you have any questions?" I did! But since my boyfriend was sitting right next to me, I figured he really wouldn't appreciate me talking about our private bedroom skills with the doctor and the two PAs that were in the room with us. So, my response was simply, "No."

I did have a question, though. Can we have sex during this? Since the oncologist was telling us to be cautious to not get pregnant, that meant we could have sex... right? I really thought going into this that I wasn't going to be able to have sex for at least the chemo months, which I was worried about, since I believe sex is a huge thing in a relationship. I mean think about it: I have a port in my chest which sticks out and looks weird. I have no hair and most of the time I'm pale. I just don't feel sexy anymore, you know what I mean? Well, probably not. You would think I really wouldn't feel like doing it, especially those first four real bad treatments. Yup, I still wanted to. In fact, I wanted to do 'the deed' more then than I do now.

I have to switch gears here for a moment. On and off since this chemo garbage has been going on, I have had episodes of constant urination. I get pumped full of a lot of crap, then go in for fluids twice a week, so I should be peeing a lot. This is different. This is the urge to pee right after I've just gone. Constant peeing and pressure, people!! It would happen to me like once a week, and for a full day I couldn't stop peeing. It went away though, so I just ignored it. About two weeks ago, same thing. One day all day I would pee... oh wait a minute, the next day same thing... constant peeing! It's lasting two days now. I can still handle this. Next day, I was fine. Two days a week now I will get the urge to pee all day. Last week, only three days after my last urination frenzy, I started the all-day peeing again. This time was bad - full force with a burning sensation. I thought to myself... *for goodness sake, now I have a urinary tract infection*! That same day, I made an appointment to see my PCP. I know my body very well, so when something doesn't feel right, I don't mess around, I seek help. My PCP did a urinalysis but since it takes 24 hours to come back, I had to wait. I have to stop here. This is going to get graphic so those of you who haven't closed this book may want to now... I will give you a minute to mull it over.

My symptoms were as follows: constant urination, pressure, and a slight burning sensation. I needed to just wait until the results came back. That night, I went to the Cancer Center to get fluids and the burning sensation got worse. I was in the middle of getting fluids and crying because I was in such pain. The nurses came over and asked me what was happening and then told me to pee in a cup. They did a rapid "dip" of the urine and it came back totally normal. They also called my PCP and got the results of the urine test that she had sent out. It came back normal, no UTI. What the hell?! I left the Cancer Center so upset and in a lot of pain. I got home and just cried. The burning sensation got so intense, it took my breath away at times. My boyfriend was trying to help me, he was looking online for "home remedies." At that point I really couldn't figure out if the burning was coming when I started to pee or if when I was peeing it started to burn as the urine hit the walls of my "coolie" (as my daughters call it). I just cried and cried. Olivia asked me if I was dying, and, being very upset and angry as I was, I yelled, "No Liv, I'm not dying, my coolie just HURTS!" My boyfriend made me peppermint tea, which, as he was researching, said was supposed to help. Then he took out the milk from the refrigerator and said, "Pour this into the tub, you need to sit in it." What?! At that moment I snapped. I yelled at him and told him to stop helping me. I know, I know, I'm wicked, I realize he was just trying to help me. It does kinda make sense, I guess. When your mouth is on fire after eating a spicy hot pepper you're supposed to drink milk to cool it down. However, at that very moment, I wasn't about to sit in the 1% milk. I was still in horrible pain, it really felt like someone had lit a match to my vagina. So, what did I do? I took three Xanax, sat in bed with a half-gallon of chocolate peanut butter ice cream and ate most of it until I passed out. Now, that's a way to get milk into me. HA!

All that happened on a Friday night. I woke up Saturday feeling much better. I was still peeing a lot but the burning sensation had disappeared. On Sunday I woke up fine, no burning, no pressure, no peeing! Thank God for some relief! Until Monday came along. Here we go again! Constant peeing and pressure, this time no burning, though. So, I figured I needed to see another doctor. I made an appointment with my GYN, to see if I had a yeast or bacterial infection, which would maybe explain things. She also did a urinalysis. I had to wait another day to get my results, but when I did, I was shocked to hear that everything was negative, totally fine. Again, what the hell?! I wasn't happy with this. I wanted to know what was happening to me. My oncologist referred me to a urologist, to see if anything weird was going on with my bladder... off to another doctor!

I waited an hour to get in to see this urologist. She asked me lots of questions about how I'm handling the chemo and what's been going on with these symptoms I'm having. I explained everything from the very first urine episode to my "hoohoo" being set on fire. She did an exam, complete with an ultrasound of my bladder, which she said looked normal. She also repeated the urinalysis, she did the rapid dip as well and this time it came back looking suspicious, so she said she would send it out and see what the lab says, and if it came back positive she would call me and put me on meds. Are you kidding me? I've had three urinalyses from three different doctors in the past week and each of them came back normal, but now you're saying this looks suspicious?

Well, today is Saturday, and I haven't heard anything from the urologist, so I guess that means I don't have an infection. In the meantime, my boyfriend and I have hit a dry spell. When I say "dry spell" I mean me. Most people don't understand that chemo affects every part of your body. I certainly didn't expect all this crazy shit to happen. My skin is very dry, my eyes and mouth get very dry, and well, "downstairs" gets very dry as well. I did some research online about vaginal dryness, and found that the symptoms are burning sensation, frequent peeing, and frequent urge to pee. Also, every time I searched vaginal dryness one word kept popping up... MENOPAUSE. I'm 30, I didn't expect this to happen to me until I was at least 50! I figured, if this is happening to millions of menopausal women, there must be an easy fix for it. My mom went to the store for me and bought me Replens, which is just a water-soluble lubricant that helps relieve vaginal dryness. I tried it, and oh my God, here we go again! The burning sensation was back! I could not get into the shower fast enough to rinse this stuff out of me. I'm seriously confused and frustrated now. Which goes back to my sex life, which right now is nonexistent.

I have been through four Adriamycin and Cytoxin chemo treatments aka AC, and eight Taxol and Herceptin chemo treatments. I have four treatments left, four more weeks, and I get to have my old self back again... I hope.

Chapter 33

February 9, 2013

Ultrasounds All Day

Since my last journal, I don't have any real news about my peeing issues. So far nothing has been resolved. The urologist said my urine culture came back negative so no UTI.

I went to the Cancer Center on Monday to get my usual fluids, but I was feeling so awful, I had to see a nurse practitioner as well. I had been blowing my nose for days and coughing, and my throat was killing me, so she thought it would be best to put me on a Z-pak. By Wednesday, I was feeling a little better, but every time I would cough my chest hurt, which radiated right to my back. I was really hoping they wouldn't give me the chemo. Think about it - I'm now on an antibiotic but I'm still getting poisoned, so how is the antibiotic supposed to work if my immune system is still getting beaten down? I just don't get it.

My blood counts were okay, so my doctor gave me the chemo. I was almost done, had finished the Taxol and now was onto the Herceptin, and right in the middle of the treatment I started to get sharp pains in my chest. My mom was with me this time, and I just kinda sat in the chair quietly. My nurse came by, and I told her I was having these pains, so she immediately stopped the Herceptin and went to get a blood pressure cuff. My mom just looked at me and said, "You've been sitting there in pain and you didn't even say anything to me about it." I know my mom, and if I had told her I was having chest pains, she would have jumped out of her chair and hunted down a nurse, frantically telling them her daughter is having chest pains and they need to see me right away. I wasn't having shortness of breath, I knew it wasn't that serious, but it never happened to me before during treatment, so I was a little nervous. I waited until my nurse came by to tell her. My blood pressure was fine and my nurse said my lungs sounded clear. The pain had now gone into my right arm so I had to see a nurse practitioner and when she came in it was like a tornado hit. She had a thick Indian accent and talked very fast. She told my nurse to give me fluids and stop the Herceptin for the rest of the day. She also ordered an EKG and blood work. Everything came back fine. The chest pain had subsided, but my arm had gone from pain to numb and heavy. I ended up leaving shortly after the results came back normal.

I still had the heavy feeling in my arm all night but by the next day I was okay. Just a side note - the nights after I have chemo, I usually feel tired and my stomach feels like there's a brick in it. I wake up a bunch of times during the night because I get really warm. I usually put a cold cloth on my forehead, and am able to get back to sleep.

Friday morning, I got up and got dressed. I had all three kids with me that morning because there was a storm coming! I got everyone ready and we headed out. I dropped the kids off at my mom’s. I had to be at the Cancer Center at 9 a.m. for fluids and for an ultrasound of my kidneys. Fluids were quick, I was in and out in no time. I waited forever to get the ultrasound done, though! Ultrasounds are easy and painless, I could do ultrasounds all day! At one point, I said to the tech, "I know you can't really tell me anything but I know you see these all day, so could you just tell me if it looks normal or not?" She was nice, she said, "Honestly, I don't see anything abnormal, but I'm also going to take an ultrasound of your bladder to see if the lining looks irritated." The more pictures the better. I need to know what's causing this!

This is going to sound random and a little out of the blue, but while I was getting my ultrasound I was thinking about all this crap I have had to go through since I was diagnosed with breast cancer. I think that everyone should be able to get an MRI of their whole body once a year. Do you realize if we all got to do that, cancer could be caught early for everyone. I truly think that would decrease the amount of deaths from cancer. However, MRIs are extremely expensive and some health insurances won't cover them. Some others that do cover them still make you pay partially, and some people don't have health insurance at all, so my dream of everyone getting scanned for cancer every year will probably never come true.

Chapter 34

February 16, 2013

It's Only Been Four Months

I have been so frustrated with this urine/burning sensation that I decided to go back to my GYN and see a doctor. Let me clarify - my GYN is actually a midwife. I see midwives all the time. In fact, all three of my kids were delivered by midwives. I've never seen a doctor for any OB-GYN issues. Oh wait, I almost forgot, the results from my kidney/bladder biopsy came back completely normal. Don't get me wrong, I'm glad there is nothing terribly wrong with me, but it's upsetting to me that there isn't anything wrong, because I know something's not right with me. Does that make sense?

I waited a long time at the GYN office. I had to wait next to a pregnant woman with two little girls. They were around the same age as my daughters. However, my children wouldn't have acted the way these two did. These two little girls were laughing and I really didn't think anything of it until the smaller one went over to her mom and "whispered" (we all know children aren't good at whispering) while laughing she said, "That girl is bald." Really?! My girls would never be that rude, and if they were, I would have said something to them and made them apologize. That mom knew I heard every word her kid said. Not only that but I always have a hat on, and my hats cover my whole head. I guess I'm not fooling anyone, though. I know they are only kids but that made me feel even worse about myself.

* * * *

The midwife I saw did a full exam. I explained everything that was happening to me and after the exam she told me that she thought the Herceptin might be making me feel the urge to pee, and also be the cause of the vaginal burning sensation. She wasn't sure, though, so she was going to talk to an oncologist she knew and also to my oncologist and get back to me. That midwife also said it looks like I have vaginal atrophy and dryness. Just great, I'm only 30! She said that once I get off the Herceptin and Taxol, my body will return to normal. I have to be on Herceptin until December, so I guess just one year is better than the rest of my life.

One of my friends took me to chemo this week. It's a shitty situation but I like being able to see and catch up with my friends. I also think it's important for everyone who is close to me to really see what I have to go through. We went in to chat with my oncologist, but this time I wasn't so happy to see her. I've said before I really like my oncologist but I need answers and I'm getting fed up. I told my oncologist that I had gone to see my OB/GYN and that the midwife thought maybe this could all be stemming from the Herceptin. My oncologist shot that down immediately. My oncologist said, yes, Taxol can make your body think you're going into menopause, but that she'd never heard that it can cause urinary/burning issues like I'm having. She said she has heard that it can cause inflammation of organs, which I quickly piped up and asked, "Bladder?" She said yes, but since I had an ultrasound of my kidneys and bladder and nothing was found, my bladder couldn't be inflamed. She also said the Herceptin can cause some issues, but again she's never heard of anything I am describing. I said, "Well, just because it's not documented doesn't mean it hasn't happened to someone else out there in the world!" As I said that, I felt like the little boy in *The Santa Clause* movie: "Just because you can't see him doesn't mean he doesn't exist."

At this point, I was angry. My oncologist was worried that I would want to stop the Herceptin treatment altogether. It really never entered my mind until that conversation. I know the Herceptin is working in my favor for reducing the chances of my breast cancer coming back and I don't want to mess with that. My argument was simply that once the chemo was over, I would still need the Herceptin every three weeks, so why not change it to every three weeks now and see if it makes a difference? My oncologist either didn't understand my question or just wasn't hearing it, because her answer was, "You're here now every week for chemo, so why not just get the Herceptin in with it?" I don't like when you answer a question with a question. I could have argued this with her all day, but I chose not to. She clearly didn't understand where I was coming from. She did say that she wasn't trying to tell me to suck it up and get over the treatments, but that she really didn't have any answers for me and that we should just play it by ear. So, I said, "So, tomorrow or Friday when I feel these symptoms again (like I said, it's not every day that I feel the peeing/burning sensation), I'm gonna call you up and tell you that I'm all done." She simply said "okay". I was so angry, but I think I did a good job of holding back most of my anger, which before chemo I would not have done. Chemo really takes a lot out of you and I wasn't wasting my strength getting all hot and bothered over this. I really like my oncologist, I don't want to get in arguments with her. At the end of the day, it's my decision what I'm going to do anyway.

(Side bar just to explain... Herceptin is a monoclonal antibody that interferes with the HER2-neu receptor. Its main use is to treat certain breast cancers.)

The HER2 receptors are proteins that are buried in the cell membrane and communicate molecular signals from outside the cell to inside the cell, and turn genes on and off. The HER2 proteins stimulate cell growth. In some types of breast cancers, HER2 is over-expressed, and causes cancer cells to reproduce uncontrollably.... This is straight from the dictionary, just a little info in case you are asking what Herceptin is even for.

My oncologist called me after I left. She said she had just received a call from the midwife I had seen. My oncologist said, "The doctor you saw at your OB/GYN office admitted she was wrong, and that it is not the Herceptin causing these issues. I just want you to understand that." Yup, I get it, you guys have no clue and you don't want me to stop the Herceptin... I didn't say that out loud. My mission now is to find as many breast cancer survivors and women undergoing treatment with Herceptin and see if they have had any of these issues I'm having. I will get to the bottom of this! Also, my Oncologist gave me the name of a GYN, who is also a breast surgeon, and would like me to start seeing her from now on for gynecological visits. I'll let you know how that goes.

* * * *

Let's sum up my feelings lately... depressed. Not just because I am having all these issues but also because I don't like the way I look. When I was younger, I looked in the mirror a lot. Not just mirrors, either, anything that I could see my reflection in - microwave, the sides of my parents' oven, the porch door, even when the TV was off I would stand in front of it to see myself. My dad always said, "If you keep looking in the mirror, one day you will see the devil." That didn't scare me and I still looked in the mirror every chance I got. I avoid the mirror now. I don't see the devil like my dad said I would, but I see a woman I don't even recognize. At first, the whole bald thing wasn't that bad. I still had a pretty face. Now, the chemo has definitely aged me. I didn't look sick when this all started, but I look sick now. Makeup doesn't seem to help, although I won't leave the house without it. I have said the whole time that this is really all mental for me, I feel myself getting more and more depressed as the days go on. To me, it feels like it's been years of chemo, when in actuality, it's only been four months. Four months ago I was healthy... I was me.

Chapter 35

February 23, 2013

Proud of Myself

The last journal I wrote, you read all about the bitching I do. I have decided not to bitch in this journal. You're welcome. I had a pretty good week, I actually (knocking on wood and praying to God that I don't jinx myself) did not have any urinary or vaginal issues, this is big for me, people! I was paranoid the entire week that the peeing/burning sensation was going to come back. I searched the web to find someone else who had the same symptoms and I found not just one person but two! Two people who had the same symptoms while going through treatment for breast cancer. One of these ladies said that her oncologist told her these symptoms were because of all the meds and crap that they were pumping in her for chemo, that she needed to drink a lot to flush it out. Makes sense, so I upped the drinking. I am really proud of myself, I am the girl who would maybe have one glass of water a day because she knew she was getting fluids intravenously the next day. I just figured I didn't need to drink, but now I have been drinking almost (yes, almost, I'm trying here) a gallon a day! So either this drinking more thing has solved my problem or... so, 15 days ago, I was put on an antibiotic for my cough and sinus problem... I'm also thinking I could have had an infection "down there" that just didn't show up on the tests and maybe the antibiotic cleared that up. I don't know, I am still going to keep well-hydrated. This drinking thing isn't so bad, and I find it easier and more appealing with ice and a straw :)

My brother David, who is also another one of my favorite people, came with me to chemo this week. David and I are very close, he is eight years older than me and when I was only three or four years old, when I would get scared I would try to sleep in bed with someone who made me feel safe again. I would go to David first because his room was right across from mine. (I also tried to sleep in bed with Beth, who would make me sleep on the floor. I also slept with my mom and dad until finally they stuck a love seat in their bedroom for me so when I was scared I could sleep on that instead of in between them.) David had rules if I wanted to sleep in his bed, stuff like I couldn't bring my Winnie the Pooh in the bed, I couldn't pull his ears, I couldn't sing. Now it's funny, but back then you can only imagine how that little four-year-old felt being scared and going to her big brother for comfort and having all those rules to follow... yes, David, I'm trying to make you feel bad. My Olivia said to me, "You want Uncle David to take you to chemo because he's funny, and you will laugh a lot, right?" He really is funny and I think he was trying to make me laugh during chemo. David loves me; I know it's hard for him to see me go through this.

Chemo went smoothly, no sudden chest pains or craziness happened. I did notice a few newer symptoms last week that I brought up to the nurse. My nails hurt, hurt to touch them and hurt to open cans. When I was a kid, apparently I complained a lot, because I remember my dad sarcastically saying, "Oh, Mickey, your stomach hurts, your head hurts, you're always saying something hurts, do your nails hurt, too?" My dad's nickname for me was Mickey Mouse because I liked the Disney character. He then shortened it to Mickey and then when I got older, it turned into Mic. Well, Dad, I wish you were still alive to hear me say this - yes, my nails really do hurt!

Another symptom was that the first and second day after chemo I got headaches. I'm hoping that with all the hydrating I'm doing now, that will help with my headaches, too. Also, and this one scares me a little, I have noticed that in the morning to the afternoon, if I'm looking at small print, such as the iPod, a book, the guide on the TV, it looks like someone ran their index and middle fingers down in a straight line. It's like column blurriness. The nurse I told this to went and spoke to my doctor about these issues, but my doctor just said they are minor problems and isn't really worried about them at the moment, but if anything gets worse then to come in right away. What she was really saying is... you only have one more chemo, just get through it.

Which brings me to the best part of this whole journal. I have ONE more chemo treatment!!!!!!!!! I want to shout it from the rooftops! I'm so excited! Chemo is the absolute worst, and I've wanted to quit so many times. I'm proud to say I didn't quit, I stuck it out and it's almost behind me. Chemo can eat my dust! However, this journey is far from over.

Chapter 36

March 2, 2013

Yell from the Rooftops!

My very last chemotherapy treatment went well. My boyfriend went with me, which I think was good since he came with me to my very first chemo. It just made sense for him to come to the last one, too. We met with my oncologist first. I am still having some issues but thank the good Lord I'm not having any urinary or burning problems anymore. My nails are still hurting and looking awful; also, the numbness in my hand and arm after I have chemo is a bit scary, but my oncologist seems to think it's a positioning problem, like I'm sleeping with my neck all kinked up, which is affecting a nerve and making my arm and hand numb. Numbness and tingling in the fingers and toes are a side effect from the chemo, but thankfully, I haven't had any of that.

My oncologist did a full exam of my lymph node and breast. She didn't feel anything, but she wants me to get an ultrasound just to make sure. I also have to get an echocardiogram every three months now, because I still need those Herceptin treatments and the Herceptin can cause heart failure... It's always something!

Once we got into a "pod," I was just so happy, I actually couldn't wait to get the chemo this time. It felt awesome to say this was the last time, the very last time, that I would be getting poisoned. I was tired and hungry when we left the Cancer Center. I really wasn't in a rush to go home, though. I wanted to celebrate, to shout from the rooftops that I had completed sixteen rounds of chemotherapy! But, it was a rainy day and I physically didn't feel like having a party so we went through the Burger King drive-thru, parked in the parking lot, and ate French fries and onion rings... it was nice.

There are just no words to describe how I feel - it's almost bitter-sweet. I am so happy that I don't have to get chemo again but I still have to get treatments and have surgery and radiation. This won't be over for a long time, but at least I got through the hard part. Chemotherapy made me sick, tired, weak, it physically changed my appearance, and got me depressed, but somehow, I came out of it stronger.

Chapter 37

March 9, 2013

Chemo Works!

My final chemo treatment came and went, and normally the Thursday, Friday, and Saturday after chemo I feel very tired and just all-around crappy. Well, not this time - this time I felt great! Mostly because I knew I wasn't going to be getting poisoned again. My hair and nails will be growing back now. My immune system will get back to normal and I will actually start getting stronger. I will be me again!

My first solo Herceptin treatment was on Wednesday, and it only took about an hour. I was so worried about this because I was really afraid that the Herceptin alone would cause me to have some crazy side effects. So far so good... knock on wood!!

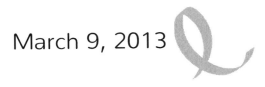

I had an ultrasound of my breast and lymph nodes on Thursday. My oncologist wanted to make sure the chemo was really doing its job. The results of the ultrasound were simple - they saw nothing! The tumors shrank so much they aren't visible on the ultrasound anymore. The lymph nodes also shrank back to normal size. I'm so happy about this! It makes me feel awesome to know that I didn't just walk through hell for nothing. The godawful chemotherapy worked!

On Friday morning I had an appointment with my surgeon to go over exactly what was going to happen during surgery. She explained that I'm going to have a lumpectomy with a sentinel node removal. In layman's terms, she's going to take out whatever is left of the tumor and also take out the tissue around where the tumor was. She's also going to remove two sections of lymph nodes.

The lymph nodes are my biggest concern. Minus the fact that I'm going to have a drain put in for at least eight days, I'm also going to have to do physical therapy, to work on the muscles under my arm. I knew this wasn't going to be easy, but now I have to worry about getting lymphoedema. The dictionary defines lymphoedema as 'a condition of fluid retention and tissue swelling caused by a compromised lymphatic system. The lymphatic system returns the interstitial fluid to the thoracic duct and then to the bloodstream, where it is recirculated back to the tissues. Tissues with lymphedema are at risk of infection.' Great, every time I get a small cut of some kind on my left arm I'm going to have to worry about my arm swelling up and getting infected. I guess it could be worse. Okay, I know it could be worse.

I think about everything constantly, my mind never shuts off. I say I want to be me again but do I really want to be 'me' again? I wasn't a bad person before I got hit with the cancer truck, but I did take life for granted. I have been saying this whole time that I really feel as though I got a second chance at life. So this time around, I'm not allowing myself to be miserable. I've decided that the things and people in my life that are making me miserable are gonna have to go! Most importantly, I'm going to "do" me. I'm going to take an hour a day and go running, meditate, get my nails done, or just do nothing... by myself! I'm going to laugh and have fun. Someday soon I will get "me" back, I'm just going to tweak myself a bit.

Chapter 38

March 19, 2013

Down and Out

I was scheduled to have another MRI two weeks ago, but I ended up rescheduling. I was having a bad day and just didn't want to do it. I remember that day, I was so upset with everything and everyone that I almost gave up. Can you imagine me giving up now? After the hard part is all done. When I came to my senses I realized how selfish that would be of me, just to give up. However, when I went back to do the MRI, I rescheduled again. I'm very claustrophobic, and I just don't want to do it. I know I have to do it, so I made an appointment for the 25th. Later when I was telling my mom about my appointment, a light went off in my head, that's my birthday. I am still going to keep the appointment though.

I have been pretty down and out these last couple of weeks. Don't get me wrong, I'm so glad the chemo is over but I just want this whole nightmare to be over! I'm waiting again and if you've been reading, you know waiting is the hardest part. My surgery isn't until April 2. I wake up every day thinking the tumors have grown back and that the cancer has spread to other lymph nodes in my body. I'm pretty sure it hasn't but I have a month from chemo to surgery, and anything is possible at this point.

Let's talk about my appearance. I HATE the way I look. Everyone I have come in contact with has said, "Oh, you look so good." Well, honestly, would you tell me I looked bad if you thought I really did? No, you wouldn't, because I have cancer and that just wouldn't be right. Believe me, I get it, because I would say the same thing if it wasn't me going through this. I hate wearing a stupid hat every time I go out. I just want my hair to grow back... now. I'm not a patient person.

I have seen and talked to a few breast cancer survivors, which makes me feel good because they got through it, they beat it, and they are healthy now, and I will be healthy again, too. I have walked straight through hell, and though I was bitching all the way through it, I had a smile on my face every time I got poisoned. I'm definitely not the strongest person in the world, but I know I got through something really big. I hope my kids grow up knowing that I did this for them, that I went through treatment after treatment, sickness after sickness. My kids are the reason I'm getting treated for breast cancer. If I didn't have those three little faces to wake up to every day, I would have given up a long time ago. I just noticed the word 'mother' is right in the middle of chemotherapy.

Chapter 39

March 27, 2013

Hot Flashes, Surgery and More...

The dictionary defines hot flashes like this: 'Also known as hot flushes, or night sweats if they happen at night, are a symptom which may have several other causes, but is often caused by the changing hormone levels that are characteristics of menopause...' Want to know how I define them? Hot flashes, otherwise known as never having a good night's sleep again!

I have been feeling pretty good since I'm not on the chemo anymore. I do get tired and the little everyday chores wear me out still, but all around I feel so much better! My newest obstacle are these damn hot flashes! I don't sleep as it is, but now it's even worse. I will get into bed very chilly, get under the warm comfy sheets, then all of a sudden it feels as if my body is burning from the inside out. My whole face gets really warm and I start to sweat, so I throw off all the sheets and put a cold cloth on my forehead. A few minutes later I'm fine, chilly again, and under the sheets. This goes on all night. I've always known about menopause and hot flashes, that someday I would have to experience it, but not at 30!

Surgery is coming up very soon. I'm very anxious to get this done. Firstly, because I just want the next step over with. I've only accomplished the chemotherapy. I need to check the rest off the list, and it seems like it's taking forever. Secondly, I'm so afraid that between now and April 2, I'm going to get sick and the surgery won't be performed as planned. I need more Xanax!

My MRI was scheduled for March 25, which coincidentally was my birthday. As you all know, I hate MRIs. I was very nervous the whole day. I wanted to cancel but I knew I really shouldn't. I took two Xanax before I left the house, and when I got to the hospital I was feeling pretty good. As I lay down on the table, I heard the tech say to the other tech, "No one is coming in with me?" Oh boy, this girl was new, and she was nervous to be in here with me by herself. She started to put the IV in my left arm. I have great veins, seriously, you can see them from ten feet away because they pop out. This tech just wasn't putting the needle in right, she was hurting me. After she kept trying to push the needle in farther, and wasn't getting anywhere, I finally said, "This is really hurting." Another tech came in the room and took over, and she also stayed in the room with me during the MRI and held my hand. That made me feel better, and everything went smoothly. I was out of there within 30 minutes.

Today I saw my oncologist, and she told me that the results of my MRI were very good; in fact, the MRI stated that there was barely anything left of my tumors. At first that was exciting to hear, but then I sat back and thought, I still need the surgery, I still need the Herceptin, I still need radiation, and I will still be on Tamoxifen for the next five years. So, I'm not really that excited anymore. I asked if I could get my port taken out early but since I'm still getting the Herceptin, she doesn't want me to get it taken out yet. The port will be in my chest, sticking out, looking like a golf ball, all summer long!

I'm a bit nervous about this surgery. I have set everything in place if in fact I don't make it out of this alive. Yes, dying is still on my brain. I got through the chemo, I'm going to have surgery and everything else, but just in case I don't make it out of this... I have made my will, I bought life insurance only a few months before I got diagnosed (good thing!), I have written letters to my loved ones, including my kids, which was very hard for me to do. Have you ever seen the movie *P.S. I Love You*? One of my favorites. The husband dies and sends scheduled letters to his wife throughout the next year. I'm not going that far, although I was thinking about it. Last Friday I was baptized. I was brought up a Baptist and in most Protestant religions we baptize as adults. Believe me, I'm not ready to die but when I do, I want to make sure I'm going up!

Chapter 40

March 27, 2013

The Pause Button

My Easter was nice and quiet. I made dinner for my boyfriend, me, and the kids. We had an egg hunt, I stuffed 143 eggs full of jelly beans and assorted candy. I gave my boyfriend the camcorder to film the kids hunting down all the eggs. At the very beginning of the egg hunt, my daughter Olivia fell and hurt her knee. My boyfriend thought he had paused the camcorder so we could tend to Olivia, however he must have hit the wrong button because when we played it back that night, we saw that he filmed Livvy's fall and paused the whole egg hunt. I was really mad when we watched it back and the egg hunt was missing. It was a mistake and he apologized but I don't think he really understood why I was so upset. See, I asked my boyfriend to work the camcorder instead of me doing it for a reason....

My surgery is on Tuesday, and I'm very scared. If you remember, at the beginning of all of this, I said, "I can do surgery all day." Well, I see it this way: I went through chemo and it sucked and it was hard and all I wanted was to get through it so I could have surgery. Now that surgery is staring me in the face, I want to run in the other direction. I'm very nervous because I have heard some really scary stories. Not stories just about breast cancer but stories about surgery in general and the crazy and horrible things that can and do go wrong. I am scared that I won't come out if this, that something will go wrong and I will die.

I wanted my boyfriend to record the egg hunt because I knew he would film me as well as the kids. He would have recorded me holding Landon's hand taking him to find eggs. He would have recorded me cheering the girls on as they spotted more and more eggs. He would have also recorded me, just me, smiling in the camera. I wasn't mad at him because he made a mistake and pressed the wrong button on the camcorder. I was upset because it will be a memory lost. If I die during or shortly after surgery, my son will never remember me. I'm not so sure my daughter Alaina would even remember me in another ten years either, she's only six. My daughter Olivia would, though, she is old enough and it surprises me now how much this kid remembers from when she was very little. I want them to be able to put home movies on and see their mom interacting with them, seeing how much I love them. The girls have a lot of home videos from when they were little, they watch them all the time. I have only recorded one video so far of Landon and I'm the one taking the video so he will only be able to hear my voice when he's old enough to watch it. This video of Livvy's fall from Easter also has me and Landon dancing on it. I propped the camcorder up on the fireplace one day so I could be in the video with Landon. If something does go wrong, at least he will see that he got to dance with his mommy.

I have said this before, I'm not afraid to die, I'm afraid for my children growing up without their mom. I don't want them to hurt because of me. Olivia would be affected the most since she's the oldest and has been with me the longest.

I wanted to see everyone within the few days before my surgery. I'm not going to put anyone on the spot so I'm not going to name names but I did ask one of my siblings if they wanted to come over for dinner the night before my surgery and they kinda gave me the runaround, busy schedules, blah blah. Then I asked another sibling if they wanted to come see me the night before my surgery, too, and that one said, "Why? I don't think it's going to be that big a deal." So I stopped asking. I love my family, and if I do happen to die on the table, they will receive letters from me. If I have learned anything from this, it's simple... MAKE time to spend with the people you care about, have fun and enjoy your life, because it could can be taken away from you sooner than you think.

Chapter 41

April 5,2013

Surgery

"It's not too late, we can still go home." That's what I said to my boyfriend when we got to the hospital the day of my surgery. I was very nervous, as you're all aware.

I had to be at the hospital for 8:30 Tuesday morning. Of course. there was a ton of traffic and we were about 20 minutes late but we got there. I had to have a mammogram done first. They needed to see where my "markers" were, so they could slip a couple wires in my boob. This helped the surgeon know exactly where my tumors were because they are not visible anymore. The wire part hurt, and it seemed like it was taking forever. Once they were done, I had another mammogram, I guess to make sure the wires were in the right spot?

My surgeon had three surgeries to do that morning. I had to wait about an hour after my mammogram as I was surgery number three. A nurse came and got me to take me into pre-op, where I was prepped with an IV and got to meet with everyone that would be assisting in my surgery. I Remember telling my boyfriend again, "It's still not too late to make a run for it." At that moment my surgeon came in and told us unless I have an evil twin, I wouldn't be getting out of this surgery.

After I was all prepped and ready for surgery a nurse rolled me into the operating room on a stretcher. I don't remember much after that. I remember seeing my surgeon; she was holding my hand as the anesthesiologist put the gas mask over my face. I started crying and that is all I remember.

I know from working in the OR that the nurses must have woken me up once surgery was over, but I don't remember that. The first thing I remember was seeing my mom. She had gotten to the hospital when I was still in surgery. I know a nurse was with her I just don't remember who she was or what she was saying. I heard they moved me around a couple times to find me a bed but again I don't remember any of that.

The first night was bad. The nurses told me if I needed to pee to call them and they would help. So, that's what I did. A CNA came and helped me out of bed and into the bathroom. The CNA said call me when you're done. I figured she was outside the door waiting for me. Nope! So, I said, rather loudly "I'm done." And no answer. So, I said screw this and got up myself, washed my hands, and strolled myself and the pole I was hooked up to that had fluids and meds running into my IV, to my bed... in the dark... without my GLASSES!!! When I got to my bed I was all tied up with the pole, I couldn't even lay down on the bed because I had all the wires that were hooked to my IV in my hand and the pole all tangled up. Again, no glasses... I couldn't see to untangle myself. I found the call button on my bed and asked for a nurse to come help me. At this point I'm in pain, I'm all tangled up and can't see! I was crying and I kept seeing my nurse go back and forth in the hall telling me one minute. 20 minutes later a different nurse came in and helped me. The CNA had failed to show me where the button was in the bathroom to call her when I was done. I was so mad, I wanted to walk out of that hospital, pole and all. I got back into bed and tried to sleep. I didn't get much sleep because a nurse would come in every two hours to check on me. The next morning, I was starving. Breakfast came and honestly, all I wanted was a bagel or toast. They brought me a slice of ham and two very soggy pieces of French toast.... No thank you! Another CNA came in my room and saw I wasn't eating so he brought me some toast and hot tea which I then spilled all over me by accident. it was so hot, I had welts on my stomach where I spilled the tea. Not a very good start to recovery.

Since I had lymph nodes removed under my left arm, I now have a drain attached under my arm, which needs to be emptied three times a day. It looks gross. It fills up with blood and grossness, but it should only be in for about ten days. I also have to take an antibiotic to reduce the risk of infection. I ended up staying in the hospital overnight for two nights. The first night was awful (as you read) but at least I had the room to myself. The next night was worse, I had a roommate and she had family members that called her throughout the night. The nurses came in to check on her every two hours as well and there was just a curtain separating us so when her light flipped on I was woken up! I really wanted to go home. Everyone told me I should stay another couple of nights, because I have three small children that will need me to be Mom when I get home, and I should stay in the hospital to get some rest but I wasn't getting any rest in that room!

I understand why the doctors wanted me to stay a couple more days. Being home, I just feel I should be doing things, so I overexert myself, but my kids need me. Even though I feel pretty crappy, I'm excited to have the surgery over and done with. Now I can cross off two things on the cancer list!

Chapter 42

April 12, 2013

Tell It Like It Is

The last week recovering from surgery hasn't been as awful as I thought it was going to be. The first few days after I came home, I was very sore and barely could move my left arm, but as the days have gone by I have been able to move my arm almost out straight, lined up with my shoulder. The pain has subsided, but it's still very sore under my arm. I'm supposed to be resting, really not supposed to be doing too much, however, I really don't know how to rest. I'm still carrying my one-year-old, still doing laundry and dishes. I vacuumed a few times but I have been putting more weight on my right arm than my left. It's not that I don't have help, I do have help, I just can't sit still... I probably do have ADHD.

The drain is pretty much in my armpit. It comes out as a long thin tube and is attached to something that looks like a grenade. It works like a turkey baster. I have to squeeze the grenade so there isn't any air in it. Doing this makes like a suction, so the fluid from where my lymph nodes were can drain into it. I empty it out three times a day and record the amount of fluid. My surgeon said that once the fluid is down to 30cc in a 24-hour period that I could get it taken out.

My appointment to review the pathology from my surgery was on Friday, so between Wednesday and Friday I was a total mess. Nervous because I was going to get the big news... Was my surgeon able to get all the cancer out in surgery? Do I have clear margins? Will I need more surgery? DO I STILL HAVE CANCER??

The rest of my life and what I choose to do with it rested in whatever my surgeon told me on Friday afternoon. I was very nervous. My brother David told me once that the sooner I went to sleep, the sooner the next day would come. He probably said that to the four-year-old Corey one night when she was scared and pulling his ears. All I wanted to do on Thursday was go to sleep, I just wanted to wake up Friday morning and go to the surgeon's office. Hope for the best but prepare for the worst, I have done this. I have prepared myself for the worst. This time if I do hear bad news, I'm not going to cry hysterically like I did the very first time I walked into my surgeon's office.

Friday came and my mom and I went to my surgeon's office. The breast navigator was there to meet us. Mom, me, an intern, and my surgeon all piled into a little exam room. My surgeon pulled, and I'm serious when I say she pulled out my drain... that hurt. You know when a magician pulls out a handkerchief from a hat? He just pulls and pulls and pulls and keeps getting the never-ending hanky. That's how I saw my surgeon pulling out my drain. Of course it didn't really happen that exact way.

My surgeon is a tell-it-like-it-is woman, which is why I like her. I, myself, am a tell-it-like-it-is woman. She explained that all of the invasive cancer was gone from my breast. YAY! Normally, the surgeon tries to get a two-centimeter margin around where (in my case) the cancer was. Since I'm a small chested woman, she only took one centimeter around. She wanted to save as much of my boob as she could without distorting it. The margin came back clear; however, the "insurance policy" is two centimeters, so I may have to have a little more surgery just to get that extra centimeter. I won't know for sure until next Thursday when the tumor board meets and reviews my case. The surgeon said that since I'm having radiation, I may not need the extra surgery, but again, it's up to the tumor board. I also found out that I was at Stage 2b to begin with but ended up being a Stage 2a. My surgeon removed 18 lymph nodes and only one was positive for cancer.

My mom and I asked if this meant that I am cancer-free and because my surgeon is tell-it-like-it-is, she said, "No, I can't tell you you're cancer-free because I don't know. These little cancer cells could be traveling around your liver and I wouldn't know that for sure." This made me a bit worried and upset. However, she went on to say that this was the reason they gave me the chemotherapy first, to knock out any potential cancer cells anywhere else in my body. Also, the reason why I will still be receiving Herceptin treatments until December, getting radiation and being on Tamoxifen for five years is to keep the breast cancer from reoccurring. I know she can't tell me, "You're cancer-free." She said, "We say you're cancer-free when you die of a heart attack at age 99." I do know that I heard her say load and clear, I no longer have any cancer in my breast. Which is awesome!!

I really can't describe how I feel. I went through seven months of straight-up hell, mentally and physically. Chemotherapy is nothing to take lightly, people. There were some days that I was praying to God to just let me die because I felt so sick and weak. Most days, I couldn't see the light at the end of the tunnel, and I was so afraid I would die during surgery. I don't feel any different. I'm still bald, still going through treatments, still tired and I will always worry that this nightmare will repeat itself. At least now I know, breast cancer didn't beat me, I BEAT breast cancer!!!

Chapter 43

April 20, 2013

More Surgery??

This past week I have been feeling really good. The weather has been nice and I think that contributes to how I feel emotionally. I also think I feel good because I know I don't have breast cancer anymore. If you remember, when this all started last September, I wasn't ill. I was actually feeling better than I had been, I got the news I had cancer and that's when I started feeling like crap... mentally. Once I went through chemo, that's when I started physically feeling sick... and looking like death.

I will admit, I'm still bummed out. I still have to get Herceptin treatments every three weeks. I'm feeling good, my hair is growing back (slowly), and I have more energy. I don't have breast cancer anymore!! Yet, I still have to go to the Cancer Center every three weeks until December and get treatment. Ugh!! I also have to get echocardiograms every three months to make sure my heart is still keeping up with the Herceptin. I will still have this crazy-looking port until next year as well! You need to understand, my mindset right now is, I had five months of chemo, I had surgery... no more breast cancer... I'm done!! I know it's not that easy, though.

I met with the radiology department this past week as well. No joke, I met with the whole department. Two secretaries, a radiology nurse, a student, and two different doctors. I thought this was going to be a quick visit but I was there a long time. Sometimes I feel like I'm on display. A staff member (doctors, nurse, student) comes in the exam room and I have to show them the goods, then we discuss the past seven months, they leave and ten minutes later, a different staff member comes in and we do it all over again. This happened four times, and the last time the door opened, all of them came in and discussed "the radiology plan." However, their plan came to a complete halt when I said, "My surgeon is still waiting to meet with the tumor board to see if I will need surgery again." It was actually comical, you should have seen their faces! I wanted so badly to say, "You got my name right, but did you read anything in my chart?" I didn't say it, I was good. They immediately starting rummaging through the chart to see what I was talking about.

A couple of days later, the tumor board met to discuss my case. I ended up calling the PA to see what was said. She told me that the tumor board kept going back to my case to discuss more and more (never a good sign). She said that since I am young (I'm getting tired of hearing that), the tumor board thinks my surgeon should go back and take out the rest of the tissue needed to get the full 2cm margins, this is just precautionary, there are no more cancer cells in my breast. However, my surgeon is on the fence. See, I'm a small-chested person, and if she needs to go back and take more tissue, then I'm probably going to have to get a mastectomy done. I think my surgeon feels that since I'm going to need radiation anyway, that putting me through a mastectomy will just cause me emotional grief that I really don't need. She also did a really good job. I'm not completely healed yet but I still look normal, and she told me she needed to plump up my breast with stuff (not like cotton balls, with my actual tissue) so it still looked normal. In fact, I actually like this boob better than the other boob.

My surgeon wants me to meet with the genetics department. Since I came up negative for the BRCA gene, there is other testing that can be done to see if I come up positive for any other breast cancer genes out there. Depending how quickly we can get that done will determine if I really need more surgery or not. I just don't want to stop, I did the chemo, the surgery and I'm doing the Herceptin. Next step is radiation, let's go already! Keep the ball rolling! I feel like I'm at a standstill again... to be continued!

Chapter 44

April 28, 2013

Herceptin... Friend or Foe?

I can't stress to you how much I hate the way I look. I have said before, I am a vain person, I just can't help it! The week before last was really bad for me and I blame the Herceptin for this. I had Herceptin the Wednesday before last Wednesday. That week was really good for me, the weather was nice, I felt good, I thought I looked pretty good, I was happy. Two days after I had Herceptin I was ready to throw myself off a bridge! I had diarrhea for five days, I had to take Imodium all five of those days. My nurses and doctors say that Herceptin isn't chemo, even though it says CHEMO right on the bag. They say Herceptin doesn't cause any side effects... yeah okay, I beg to differ! I've also been crying nonstop. I can't look in the mirror without being overwhelmed with tears! I'm having a weird kind of skin problem. It started last month, under one of my eyes. I thought it was just wrinkles at first but then it got puffy and then it went under both eyes. Now the puffiness is gone but it looks like a patch of dry skin or a combination of wrinkles and dry skin. I don't know but it's really getting to me.

I know it doesn't seem like such a big thing to be wicked upset over, but think about it. Most days I feel like crap, I'm always tired, my hair is on the re-growth stage, which is just bullshit. The front isn't growing in, I look like an old man that only had the hair around the sides of his head. I look in the mirror and see a bald, tired, weak woman, now with a skin problem. This has really made me go crazy. I'm very self-conscious about this, I feel like every time I talk to someone, all they are doing is staring at this problem under my eyes. Plus, the constant peeing is back. Last year at this time, I was pretty and energetic, and I didn't ever think that in a year's time I would have been put through chemo and surgery for breast cancer. I just want to be myself again!

The visit with my surgeon went well. We discussed the need for more surgery. She told me it was my decision if I wanted her to operate again or not. My mom went with me. I really didn't know what to do. It's really more for precaution, they like to get the 2cm margins and since my surgeon wasn't able to get it the first time, the tumor board suggested they go back in and get the whole 2cm. My mom said, "If the breast cancer was to come back, you don't want to say to yourself, I should have had them go back and get the rest of the margins." She's right - knowing myself, I would be lying awake every night worried that the breast cancer is going to come back because I didn't have them clear the 2cm margins. So on to surgery again!

This time, surgery won't be as bad as the last time. I won't have a drain since they are just cutting into my boob this time and not touching the nodes, thank the heavens! I also won't have to stay overnight. The last surgery took four hours, but this one won't take as long.

I went to a salon to see if they could help me with the wrinkled puffiness under my eyes. The esthetician said she thinks the chemo made the skin under my eyes very thin and dry. I was trying to cover it up with tons of makeup. She told me the makeup was making it worse and I needed to moisturize. She also said, "Do not apply makeup to that area." What?! No makeup under my eyes?! I'm not really happy with that since I have very dark circles on top of this wrinkled mess. However, I'm going to try it for a few days. If anyone asks what happened to my eyes, I'm just going to say, "You should see the other guy!"

Chapter 45

May 8, 2013

Seize the Day

Carpe diem... seize the day! Words I believe everyone should live by. I'm not a spur-of-the-moment kind of girl. I'm a planner, I need to know everything, I need to prepare for everything, and I don't like surprises. So, you can imagine my insanity when I heard my diagnosis last year, the fact that I had no time to prepare for it and I had no idea what was going to happen to me made me a little crazier than I already was. Well... no more! I'm going to seize the day from now on.

I have talked about my dad a little bit. I loved my dad and I miss him. I listened to him, I did what he told me to do. I truly believe that the last four years of my life would be completely different right now if my dad had been alive. I think I took more from my dad than I did my mom. I'm not talking about personal items, I'm talking about behaviors. Which is unfortunate for me, because my dad was a miserable person. He didn't trust anyone, and he was very moody. Don't get me wrong, he was a good dad... to me. I believe behaviors are learned. I think I learned to be miserable, to always see the glass half-empty. I had 27 years with my dad, so attempting to change the way I see life now is pretty difficult, especially when everyone in my life knows "that Corey" and is used to her. Either likes her or doesn't like her.

Once I got diagnosed with breast cancer, everyone told me to stay positive, that this disease is 90% mental. Was I positive through the last seven months of this crap? No, I wasn't, I was miserable. Honestly, most days I should have had a "get out of misery free card," but I didn't. I spent seven months miserable and upset because I thought the worst, I could never see the glass half-full, but look at me now... I survived. Most of the chemo days I didn't feel well, so the misery set in even more. I look back on it now. I was sick and felt like shit, and I could have died. I could have lost my whole life and my kids would have remembered me not only being sick but being miserable and upset, too. Twenty-seven years from now, my kids will be talking about me to someone they know, and I don't want them to say "my mom was always miserable." I want to be happy, and more importantly, I want my kids to know and see that I am happy. I know "positive Polly" doesn't show up overnight but I'm going to try my best because life really is too short to be any other way.

I have surgery scheduled on the 28th, to go in again and get the 2cm margins. Do I really want to do this? My surgeon told me at the last visit that when she really wants me to follow through with something (like chemo or the first surgery), she will tell me out straight. She didn't tell me this time, she said it was up to me. Going under anesthesia can cause nerve damage, aspiration, and heart problems, which I never thought of the first time, but now that I might need to do it again, these are the things I need to take into consideration, and also because I'm Googling again. I know, I need to get off the internet. People, I told you, positive Polly doesn't happen overnight. I think I have come to realize that bad things just happen, and if it's meant to be, I won't be able to stop it even if I try.

Chapter 46

May 17, 2013

I'm Sold!

I'm getting tired of going to the Cancer Center. I was supposed to have Herceptin treatment the Thursday before Mother's Day, but I rescheduled. There was no way I was going to feel crappy on Mother's Day, especially since I was cooking for my family.

When I was having chemotherapy, I was there each week because I knew it was the only option and I knew it was working. I don't actually know that the Herceptin is working. So I will continue to go every three weeks (or four) and get it done. I think I freak myself out before having Herceptin. I know I don't feel well for five days or so after I have it. I was very nervous and just didn't feel well the whole day before having Herceptin. The last couple of weeks, I've felt good, I just don't want to have treatment anymore. Sitting in those God awful brown polka dotted recliners, having cancer is depressing enough, why on earth do you want to go into a place to get treated for cancer when the establishment looks just as bad as you feel. If I could "re-face" the Cancer Center, it would be colorful and fun. Everything there is brown. Brown walls, brown floors, and brown chairs. My chemo nurse said she could just see it on my face, that it was getting harder and harder for me to get myself to the Cancer Center for these treatments. Seven more months to go, so I guess I just have to keep it in my head that it's not forever and will be over soon. By Christmas, I will have completed chemo, two surgeries, radiation and Herceptin, I can't wait!

That's right, I said "completed two surgeries." I talked to my oncologist, and I explained how I really didn't want to have more surgery, especially since my surgeon is leaving the decision up to me. My oncologist said, "The tumor board said you need more surgery, so that's it, that's the decision." I also explained to her that my surgeon wasn't pressing the issue. My oncologist explained that I have DCIS - Ductal carcinoma in situ (DCIS) is the presence of abnormal cells inside the milk ducts in the breast. DCIS is considered the earliest form of breast cancer, it is noninvasive, meaning it hasn't spread out of the milk ducts to invade other parts of the breast. I guess you wouldn't get treated for DCIS unless you have the breast cancer gene, because it's pretty much harmless. Because I've already had invasive breast cancer, they want to remove the DCIS in case it decides, in 10 or 20 years, to become invasive. See, my surgeon didn't explain it like that to me. My oncologist also said, "If it were me, I would have more surgery." So, that's it, I'm sold!

Chapter 47

May 23, 2013

I Have Hair!

Surgery is in five days!! I'm a little nervous, just because I will be under the knife again, but for the most part I really haven't been thinking about it too much... and if you know me, you're saying, "Yeah, right!"

I was hoping the genetic test results would be back by now but no such luck. As I said, I was negative for the BRCA gene, but because I'm young, the doctors felt they should do more gene testing. Go in for a deeper look, I guess. I really don't expect to be positive for any of the breast cancer genes. I still think this was just a freak thing that happened to me.

I am very happy to report that my hair is growing back! I think it's growing back pretty fast, which is unusual for me. I don't remember this but when I was around four or five, I had shoulder-length hair (I've seen pictures). I guess I would complain a lot when my mom would brush it, so she thought having short hair would be better for me and had it all cut off.

It was cute, but VERY short. Mom says it took two years to grow back! Hopefully, it won't take two years to have cute hair again!

"I have heard there are troubles of more than one kind. Some come from ahead and some come from behind. But I've bought a big bat. I'm all ready you see. Now my troubles are going to have troubles with me!"

˜Dr. Seuss

Chapter 48

May 31, 2013

Wrinkled Mess

Surgery went well, or so I'm told. My mom took me to the hospital and waited a few hours until I was done. I don't remember much. Just before the surgery, I had to change into a johnny, Ted (anti-embolism) stockings and ugly green socks. I also had to meet with the nurse and anesthesiologist who would be with me during the surgery. I was getting nervous (yeah, I know you're not shocked), so the nurse gave me a sedative just before they rolled me into the operating room. You all know how much I love Xanax, but whatever they gave me to calm me down was way better than my Xanax. Once I was in the operating room, I had to move onto the operating table. I remember my surgeon talking to me. "Okay, Corey, we are going to get started." The tears just came out of nowhere. I was crying a lot. A nurse was holding my hand while the anesthesiologist put the gas mask over my face. My surgeon said, "Don't cry, you're going to ruin your pretty eye makeup." That's the last thing I remember. When I woke up, a male nurse was in the recovery room with me. He was nice, he brought me water and crackers and tried to make me smile. My mom got to come in with me once I got up and was able to sit in a recliner. Mom said my surgeon told her everything went well and she is confident this time that she got it all. Fingers crossed!

The day after my surgery I was pretty sore, and very tired. Beth came and stayed with Landon so I could sleep, but I didn't sleep very much. My genetic test results came back negative! This is great news, I have been saying from day one there is just no explanation for breast cancer to have happened to me, it was just a freak thing. Breast cancer doesn't run in my family and now that I know I don't have any breast cancer genes, I'm very confident that this will not happen to me again.

I have to wait about three to four weeks until I can start radiation. So, I'm thinking I will be starting in July. Radiation is six to eight, every day. I'm not looking forward to driving to Providence every day for only an hour or so, but I know it will go by fast.

Remember how I was talking about the wrinkled mess under my eyes? I went to two different makeup artists to help me cover it up. I thought it was looking okay until I noticed it was getting worse! I finally went to a dermatologist because I just couldn't take it anymore, I was really looking old and my self-esteem was dropping rapidly. The doctor looked under my eyes and said, "Are you using any new makeup?" I said, "Actually, yes, I always wore Bare Minerals, but right after I had surgery I changed all my makeup over to new stuff. Then I noticed this wrinkled mess and bought different creams and makeup that I'm using now to try to cover it up." She said, "I know what this is. It's not wrinkles. It's an allergic reaction to the makeup you used after your surgery and you have exacerbated it by using more stuff that you're probably allergic to." I saw her on a Friday, and she gave me some medicated cream and said it should be better by Monday. Well, I went out of that office thinking, *Yeah right, I had spent two months killing myself over this wrinkled mess, trying everything to get rid of it or make it look better, and she's telling me this cream is going to make it all better in three days... yeah, okay lady!* As skeptical as I was, I used the medicated cream two times a day for the three days. That Monday, I woke up, looked in the mirror, and the wrinkled mess was GONE! I had my face back!

Chapter 49

June 9, 2013

Happy and Relieved

I have Herceptin every third Wednesday of the month. I always dread having Herceptin. The doctors and nurses will tell you that Herceptin doesn't have any real side effects, that's why they don't consider it chemotherapy. Herceptin is actually classified as a chemotherapy, it just isn't horrible like the other chemos out there. With the A/C and the Taxol, I knew what symptoms I was going to have. I had the same symptoms every time I had the treatments. With the Herceptin, it's a crap shoot. I feel like I develop a new symptom every time I have it.

At last month's Herceptin, I think I was actually starting my period again... I say *think* because I really don't know. I know what you're saying: "How don't you know?" Chemotherapy stopped me from getting periods way back in December. That was the only good thing about going through all this crap. The doctors and nurses said I probably wouldn't get it back for at least a year... of course, they didn't realize who they were talking to. I'm fertile Myrtle! I actually felt like I was getting my period so I ran to the bathroom but I was only spotting, and after that I got incredible back and side pain. Then that was it, nothing else since. I told my oncologist about this and she was happy about it. She said, "Yeah, your periods could be coming back. Everyone is different and you're young (there it is again), so you may get it back sooner than we thought." I'm not happy about this. I used to have very heavy periods, but never really had pain or cramps with it. I understand my oncologist is happy because this means all the "bad" chemo is almost out of my system and I'm getting back to being healthy again. I was so hoping I wouldn't get my period back for at least a year, like the doctors had said originally. Looks like I may get it back sooner than later, but maybe I'll get lucky and I'll have really light periods now. Yeah, I know. Who am I kidding.

I saw my surgeon last week to go over the pathology results from the last surgery. She said everything looked good, the pathology results said she got a good clear margin. No more surgeries needed, PHEW. All the cancer, including the DCIS, is GONE!

I had Landon with me when I saw my surgeon. I'm glad he's so small and doesn't really understand what's going on yet. When I got home after my appointment, Landon had fallen asleep in the car. I just sat in my car and cried. Not because I was upset, but because I was happy and relieved. Going through this has been so hard. It's put an emotional weight on me, but I did it! I did the hard stuff, no one else could do it for me. I did it and it took an emotional and physical strain on my body, but now I can say it's almost over!

Herceptin for another seven months and radiation for seven weeks... it doesn't seem so bad now, I know I can do it!

Chapter 50

June 20, 2013

Herceptin Strikes Again

Okay, let's see, what can I bitch about?

* * * *

Well, for starters... have I mentioned I hate this port?! Ugh... summer is here and I want to wear my cute sleeveless and halter tops. Nope, the port has put the kibosh on that! I had to buy some new tops to cover it. I feel like I'm on *Star Trek Deep Space Nine*, hitting the button on my shirt every time I want to command the *Enterprise*. It just sticks out. My nurses keep telling me, "You're really thin, so that's why it sticks out so much. If you were heavier, it wouldn't be so noticeable." They should have told me to gain weight before all this started, it would have given me an excuse to eat packages of Oreos and Hostess cupcakes by the box. Of course, I wouldn't have done that, I have a bit of a weight issue which stems back to my dad but that's another story for another day. I also bought a new bathing suit. It's ugly and striped but at least it covers my port.

Herceptin strikes again. The day after my last Herceptin treatment, I woke up with a terrible migraine. I have a history of migraines but I really only get them when I'm pregnant. No worries, I'm not pregnant. Right before I get a migraine, my vision goes screwy. Do you know what a Mylar balloon is? Everything I look at turns into a Mylar balloon and floats up, then goes completely gray. This only last for about 20 minutes to a half hour. I know, weird, right?! The first time this happened to me, I thought I was going blind, and it totally freaked me out. I went to the eye doctor and the neurologist right after. Nothing wrong with my eyes, or my brain - this is called an ocular migraine. It happens right before the migraine comes on, like a warning. Then I get hit with a massive migraine that lasts for two days. I'm pretty sure it was just a coincidence, since I've had Herceptin 16 times so far and only one migraine. I have also noticed that when I'm in hot water or if I'm in the sun, I get a prickly sensation in my arms and legs. I've had this sensation for a while now, so I really need to remember to bring this up to my oncologist the next time I see her.

I've been feeling pretty good. Except of course, for the stomach issues... story of my life! I mean, I still have some bad days, but things are getting better. When I turned 30, I said my thirties are going to be great. Then I got breast cancer and I thought, really?! My thirties WERE going to be good and this is what I start off with?! This is my second chance at life. I have a second chance to make my life better, to be happy, and not take it for granted, because I know exactly what it feels like to almost lose it. So I say, my thirties CAN still be good!

Fifteen weeks since my last chemo, and I can almost do a fohawk with my hair!

Chapter 51

July 5, 2013

Phase 3

Breast cancer sure isn't something you can just shake off. I didn't realize how involved this whole process was going to be. I thought, chemotherapy... yes. Surgery... yes. Radiation... yes. Herceptin? Tamoxifen? What the hell? I have five phases of breast cancer. That doesn't mean everyone has five phases. Some people get lucky and only have two phases, like surgery and radiation, while others out there might have more than five phases, or worse... some have not made it through all of their phases.

I have completed two out of the five phases so far - chemo and surgery. I was up all night the night before I went in for the "mapping" (as they call it) for radiation. You should know me by now - I couldn't help but be nervous. I know it's nothing like chemo, but the unknown scares me. When I got to the radiology department, I had to see the doctor first. He knew I was nervous, but explained that radiation is nothing like chemo. I won't get nauseous or have any of the horrible symptoms that I had during chemo. The doctor did say I will get tired, but it's cumulative, and I might have some skin irritation down the line. I asked him if going through with the radiation was something I really needed to do. I figured since I already did five months of chemo, had surgery twice, am currently having Herceptin treatments and will be on Tamoxifen for the next five years, did I really need to do radiation? The doctor explained that I have a 40% chance of the cancer coming back, so radiation is needed in order to lower that percentage. Then he said, "We want to make sure you live another 10-20 years." Ten to twenty years?? That's it?! Does he think I'm 60? Everyone I've seen along this journey says how young I am, that I have so many more years to live, and now this guy is telling me he wants to insure I live ten to twenty years? Umm buddy, can you insure I live another fifty years instead?!

The radiology tech took me into the room to have a CAT scan. She positioned me with my left arm above my head and told me to stay very still. Then the doctor came in to make sure I was positioned correctly, and after that they both left the room. It was time to have the CAT scan. I don't mind CAT scans, they don't make me nervous like MRIs do. Once the CAT scan was over, the tech came back in and said, "Almost done, I just need to tattoo you." Hmmm... I was told about the tattooing from a couple other survivors. It is an actual tattoo, done with ink and a needle. Nothing pretty or cool to look at, just a blue dot in three different places on my chest. The radiologist does this so that when I go in to have radiation, they won't have to scan me every time. I'm already "mapped" out. It's permanent. Also, in case I end up having a reoccurrence down the line, they will know exactly what part of my breast was radiated.

Radiation is every day, Monday through Friday. I will have it for a total of six-and-a-half weeks. All summer!! I'm not looking forward to this but I know it's necessary. There were so many times through this hell that I just wanted to give up, but I didn't. The hard part is over... onto phase three!

Side bar... I'm very excited that my hair is growing, I have been putting a headband on. I know I don't really need the headband for any real purpose but it makes me feel girly.

Chapter 52

July 21, 2013

The "Plan"

Radiation is supposed to be a cake walk, or so I have been hearing. I guess compared to chemo it is. I went in for what I thought was just a "hello, let's get your schedule together and goodbye." Not so. I had to do a "dry run," get undressed, put the ugly johnny and robe on, and sit and wait for 15 minutes until they called me in. Then I was positioned on a cold table, with my bad arm up (when I say bad arm I mean the one that had all the lymph nodes taken out), and told not to move for a few minutes while they took an X-ray. I was told that radiation will take about 10 minutes and it opens real early in the morning until late at night, so scheduling will never be a problem. Again, not so. The girl who does the scheduling was very nice, but I could tell she was getting aggravated with me when I kept telling her that I have three children, and unless she wants to watch them while I'm having radiation, there is no way I can come in at 7 a.m. every morning. What happened to "scheduling will never be a problem?" They couldn't fit me in their schedule this week, so radiation will be put on hold until next week. I'm fine with that, I actually really don't want to have the radiation at all. Like everything else in my life, I seem to complete the hard stuff, but it's the easy stuff that I walk away from. I realize I can't walk away this time, but honestly, I have no desire to go to the Cancer Center every day for the next six-and-a-half weeks!

My radiologist thought he should go over the plan with me. The plan, simply put, was that he went over my X-rays and such and tried to get as much of my lungs out of the radiated area as possible, except he still had a lot of lung in this area, so he needed more time to make sure only a little bit of lung would be radiated and not most of it. Have I told you how much this whole cancer thing sucks?! Well... it does!! I'm 31, I should not be going to a radiologist discussing my left lung being an issue for radiation, let alone going to a radiologist at all! I keep thinking things like, *what did I eat*? Or what was I exposed to? Did I work somewhere that could have exposed me to something awful? Maybe I should have never gone on birth control pills? Maybe when I was a kid I didn't eat enough vegetables? Did I stand in front of the microwave too much? I just keep going over my life, over and over to figure out, why me? Then I think, if I knew 10 years ago that when I turned 30, I would be diagnosed with breast cancer, would I have done anything differently? And if I had done things differently, would I still have had breast cancer?

I can still hear the therapist I used to go to saying, "How are you feeling today, Corey?" ANGRY! That's how I'm feeling! I'm so angry that this cancer crap happened to me, and that even though I don't have breast cancer anymore, I still have to be treated for it for another five years! This is my life now, breast cancer is going to follow me for the rest of my life... yeah, I'm angry.

Chapter 53

July 23, 2013

Radiation

Radiation was very interesting... I scanned my little blue card that I was given the last time I was there, went directly into the locker room, and changed into an ugly johnny and blue robe. Then I paced up and down the hall because I couldn't find the waiting room... no worries, the janitor pointed me in the right direction. As I'm sitting in the waiting room, half-dressed with other patients fully dressed all around me, I'm thinking, *get to know these people, Corey, because you're going to* be *seeing them every day at the same time for the next six-and-a-half weeks, these are your people.* Of course, they are all much, much older than me and staring at me like I'm a prodigy.

The radiology tech came and got me from the waiting room, then she and two other techs positioned me on the table. "The doctor made some slight changes, so we are going to take some more X-rays before you get the radiation." Changes? Great. How about we change this whole situation and I wake up from this horrible nightmare that I've been having for the last 10 months. I had to stay on the cold table in a weird position for 25 minutes. My neck was killing me, because I had to keep my body flat but turn my head up and all the way to the right. I also had a fan blowing directly onto my face, which then caused my eyes to tear. I really wasn't crying, it was all that damn fan. After they took the X-rays, the tech came back in and told me to keep still and that I was going to see the machine move all around me, that was the radiation part. It was done very quickly. I kept shutting my eyes when I could see the machine move over my face. I was afraid I would get the radiation in my eyes or something.

I could not get off that table fast enough. I just wanted to get out of there. However, I had to sit down with the nurse and go over a few things.

Go over the radiation process and side effects AFTER they had already given me the radiation?! The nurse just told me not to use lotions on the radiated area, that they were only radiating where the tumors were. So, not to be worried about wearing eye protection or a lead apron, so I guess I can keep my eyes open. Then she said, "You can go in the sun, but wear sunscreen. You can't go in a pool or get the area wet, though." Excuse me? I can't get the area wet? Can I take a shower?! The nurse told me, yes, I can take a shower, but I can't go in a pool with chemicals or in the water at the beach or a pond. That was it, I lost it. I was totally fine and composed and then the tears started flowing. "Oh honey, are you crying because I said you can't go in a pool?" Are you kidding me?! NO! I don't care about the pool or the beach! I'm crying because I am so done with this shit! I'm crying because I want my life back! "Would you like to see the doctor or visit with the hospital psychologist?" Oh my God, get me out of here!

I left soon after that. I got in the car and called up a friend who took this same journey a few years ago. I told her that I totally broke down and told her about what the nurse said. She simply said, "Corey, she hasn't been through it and she doesn't really get it, no one does unless they have been though it themselves." My friend is totally right, no one will ever really understand what this has, and is, doing to me. So far radiation has been very emotional for me and it's only been two days! Another six weeks to go!

Chapter 54

July 31, 2013

In a "Mood"

I really like the Cancer Center, I like all the nurses and the doctors... however, the radiology department is a whole other ball game! "Radiation is a breeze." "Radiation is so easy." "Radiation will fly by." This is what I have been hearing. Apparently, these people don't know who I am... I attract the negative... plain and simple!

I have to see the radiologist on Mondays, so it makes the time there a little longer than usual. Monday, I went in and changed into the ugly johnny, got called in, positioned myself on the table, and the techs came in to fix me so I was lined up with the machine. Okay, I'm ready! Now my arm, the bad arm, was put in a "cuff" above my head in a very awkward position throughout the radiation treatment, which should only take about five minutes. As I'm lying there and have counted 60 Mississippis five times, yet I'm still lying on this machine, I'm wondering why it's taking longer than usual. I noticed that the machine was hovering over my head, shaking back and forth for a long time. All I could think of was that this machine was going to break down, fall on my head and crush me to death.

Meanwhile, my left arm still in the cuff was going completely numb and hurting, so the tech came in and said, "Oh, I'm so sorry, the machine isn't working, I don't know why. Just keep still, we are trying to get it to work, a few more minutes." I was getting really mad... so four songs playing on the radio in the background go by, which is what, like four minutes a song, so we will say another 16 minutes went by and now I'm on the verge of tears because my arm is killing me and my neck is shaking so much because again I'm in an awkward position. Finally, after swearing out loud and threatening to jump off the table, the tech came in and said, "Okay, you can take your arm down now, I'm really sorry but we weren't able to give you the radiation because the machine isn't working." Are you F%#@ing serious?! "Just go sit in the waiting room, because it's Monday and you need to still see the doctor." Oh, I was angry!!!! My arm hurt so bad. I went into the waiting room and waited another 15 minutes until a nurse came out and brought me into the room to see the doctor.

Oh, this nurse. Now I was already upset because I had been in the machine for over 20 minutes and my arm was really hurting. I wasn't happy. This nurse says, "Hi, we haven't met yet, but I'm one of the nurses, you don't look very... ummm, are you okay?" So, I said, "Well, my arm is really hurting, I was in the machine way too long."

The nurse says, "Oh? How long were you in the machine? Was your arm hurting before you came here?"

"I was in there at least 20 minutes and no, my arm was fine before I came here." So she says, "Oh, why were you in the machine so long? That's not normal. Do you normally take something for your arm pain? I'm just not sure why you have this pain?"

I said, "Apparently, your machine isn't working, that's what the tech told me. And my arm hurts because I don't have all my lymph nodes anymore, so when it's up in an awkward position it starts to hurt. I don't take anything for the pain. I've been here a long time and I just want to leave." I don't think I was being rude at all. The nurse then said, "Well, since you have been here a while, I will have the doctor come see you instead of you seeing the resident first." Okay! A minute later, the door opens and that nurse peeks her head in the doorway and says, "I told the doctor that you're in a mood, so to see you ASAP so you can go home."

Then she closed the door. I'm in a mood?! Well, at this point I think I deserve to be! The doctor came in a few minutes later, apologized and asked if I had any questions. If I did have any questions, I had forgotten them by then. I just said, "No, I would like to leave now."

The next day when I went in, I did my thing. I lay on the table and the tech from the day before says, "Hi, I just want you to know that we fixed the machine so it will be much faster this time and I'm really sorry about yesterday." I just said, "Great, let's go," and then I start counting... Well, here we go again! Are you kidding me?! The machine stops working and my arm starts to go numb. The tech comes in and says, "I'm so sorry, I don't know what's going on, it was working fine all day, just give me a few minutes, okay?" The machine still did nothing, but two songs later, the tech came back in and said, "All done." I'm pretty sure I didn't get the dose, they just didn't want to tell me. Of course, the machine worked all day up until I came in, why? Because again... I attract negativity!

Chemotherapy was awful but radiation just plain sucks!

Chapter 55

August 14, 2013

On My Soap Box

Last time we talked, I was clearly upset with the whole radiation process. You will be happy to know it has gotten so much better. Is my nose growing, because I'm lying. I shouldn't say that, it hasn't gotten any worse, so I guess that's better? Two weeks down and four and a half more to go!

I recently read something that talked about living every day like it's their last. You know that saying, "Live like you're dying?" My question is... why would you want to live every day like it's your last?! Now, I understand why people say that... because we would HOPE you would treat everyone better, love more, enjoy every-thing life has to offer but seriously... If you knew you were going to die tomorrow, what would you do? How would you act? Seriously now, really think about it, because before I was diagnosed with cancer, my answer to this was... I would spend every last second with the people I love, I would be happy and enjoy it all!

Reality set in and I was actually faced with "I'm dying," this could be my last day on earth. Suddenly, I wasn't happy, I wasn't enjoying my life, I didn't want to see or be around the people I loved, I was angry that I had cancer and I could die and being around the people I loved was too hard for me. I was mad and upset with everyone, because they were healthy and I wasn't. It wasn't fair that for months I thought I could be dying and I wasn't going to see my kids grow up. So, really think about that saying the next time you hear it. I say... Live like you will never die. Maybe then everyone will slow down, be friendly to one another, and be happy. Because if you think you are never going to die, you won't think you will run out of time, you won't worry so much, stress so much, and maybe you will have fun with your life.

Remember when you were a small child? Did you worry about dying? Probably not. You were a kid who just wanted to play, be silly, and have fun. I think that's what we all need to do in life. I'm getting down off my soap box. Until next time... play, be silly, and have fun!

Chapter 56

August 20, 2013

Comfy Chairs and Little Boobs

Day 19 of radiation went as follows... Beep... that's the sound of me checking in at the desk. It's great, I don't even need to pretend to be friendly and say "Good, and you?" I just walk up to the desk, put my blue badge under the scanner and BEEP, my name comes up and says I'm here!

Next, go to locker room, undress from the waist up and get into the ugly johnny and blue robe.

Sit in waiting area....

I don't know what it is about radiology, but once I sit in the chairs - and these are nice chairs, fake leather, very comfy. These chairs should be up on the chemo floor. (I may make a suggestion next time I get Herceptin.) Something about being on the radiation floor just puts me to sleep.

I really don't know what it is except maybe my body is just totally exhausted from months of poisoning, having surgery, and being stressed that now when I get in the chair, I just need to rest... or the chairs are just that comfy. Either way, when I get in those chairs, my eyelids get heavy, and I really could fall asleep....

"Corey...."

And I'm up, and ready to get into the radiation machine. I asked the tech what the machine does when it's hovering over me and when the sides come out like wings on an airplane. She said the machine is adjusting to the correct measurements that they put in. Once I hear the high-pitched beep and see the red lights come on, that's when I'm actually getting the radiation. The long part is when the machine takes its sweet time configuring to my measurements. The actual radiation is probably only three minutes long. It took a little longer today because I had to have X-rays taken. The techs take X-rays once a week to insure they are radiating the right spot. I also needed a CAT scan today. I asked the doctor, why the CAT scan, and he said, "Just to make sure we don't have any surprises." This is the same doctor who told me I needed to have radiation to "make sure I live another 10-20 years." Yeah, I'm pretty sure he's just bad with words... I hope so, anyway.

The CAT scan was very awkward. At first, they had me lying on my back with my left arm to the side of my head just like I do every day when I get radiation. However, the radiologist came in, looked at the goods and decided lying on my right side, leaning ever so slightly to the left (but not leaning on anything!) with my left arm bent over and to the side of my ear with my wrist bent out and crunched in between my head on a "soft" block, with my finger slightly under my head, was the way to go! Seriously? There was no better way to do this?! How many of you are trying to get yourself in this position right now?

That wasn't even the good part. The good part of this little story is that the techs took pictures of me in this crazy position, like actual pictures... with a cell phone, so that I wouldn't forget what position I was in. Let me explain... I have to get a "boost," which is just simply "high-def radiation." I get the boost for the last seven days of radiation, in which I will have to lie in this position. These pictures will ensure that I remember what position I need to be in. Seriously, am I being punked? Please tell me Ashton Kutcher is here.

I'm Still Here

I got out of the shower tonight and looked in the mirror, really looked at myself for the first time in a long time. Don't worry, I'm not going to talk about my hair, how it's growing up and out like a chia pet, or how the circles under my eyes are getting darker by the day, no, we aren't talking about that. I have four scars, which don't really bother me, except the biggest one looks and feels weird. I noticed that my skin is changing color, which the radiologist said would happen. Half of my chest looks red and is tan. It's almost like I fell asleep in the sun, wearing a shirt that only covered one boob, you all know what that's like, right? I walked into the bedroom and said to my boyfriend, "They look different, don't they?" He said, "Yeah, one is definitely bigger than the other." Gee, thanks, hun! No, I meant the color!!

Under my left arm hurts a lot now too, probably because my little left boob is being blasted with high- powered lasers. Yes, I said little. I'm lucky to fit into a B cup, and looks can be deceiving. Victoria has all kinds of secrets ladies. Which just brings me to the question of all questions... How the hell did I get breast cancer when I hardly even have breasts! They may as well call it, fat tissue cancer!! Yes, I'm still bitter.

Chapter 57

September 7, 2013

Milestone

It's been one year since I was diagnosed with breast cancer. I remember last September 7 like it was yesterday. I was scared and angry about all this disease stuff.

Last year, I never thought I would make it out of this alive. I thought for sure I was going to die. I'm not a positive person to begin with, so giving me what I thought was a death sentence and then telling me to keep a positive attitude was not going to happen. This last year was full of me sobbing, feeling crappy, and being angry and scared. I'm not gonna lie, I'm still scared of what's next. I'm on the right train, and I'm almost at the light.

Lots of people, not just me, have problems remembering certain (important) dates. I will admit, being a mom of three, when I'm asked on the spot at the pharmacy for one of my children's birthdates, it takes me a minute or two to get it right. Since last year, I've had a few dates stick out for me. September 7, 2012... diagnosed with breast cancer. October 18,

2012... my very first chemotherapy treatment. Those two dates will forever be in my head, those were the scariest days for me so far. There is one more day that I will never forget, April 12, 2013... that was the day my surgeon told me I had beat the shit out of breast cancer! So, to all my family and friends reading this, I expect a big party next April 12. No pressure.

Monday marked another special day for me, a milestone, my 32nd and last radiation treatment! I have gone on and on about how much I hate radiation, and I am very glad to have ended it. I have to say, the first few weeks of radiation I felt tired, but since then I have felt really good. I'm not saying I could run a marathon right now because I can hardly do 15 minutes on my elliptical. I'm just glad I'm not as worn out as I thought I would be.

Chemo... check!
Surgery... check!
Radiation... check!!!!!
Herceptin... ugh, three more months....
Tamoxifen... five years....

Thankfully my Herceptin treatments will be ending in December and I can finally get this godawful port removed from my chest, which my daughter Olivia will also be happy about. She constantly asks me when it's going to come out, and my response is simply a look of "really kid, stop asking me, I don't know!!" She knows that look very well. Oh, this port, I know one thing for sure - when I get the okay to have it taken out, you won't be hearing me say, "Oh, but it's a part of me now. I feel attached to it." Hell no! I'm gonna say, "Where's the scalpel, I'll do it myself!"

Tamoxifen however, well, that will be a five-year battle. Tamoxifen is a pill, and because I am estrogen-positive I have to take it. Estrogen in my body is what drove my tumors to grow so aggressively. Tamoxifen will somewhat stop that process, so breast cancer cells won't be able to grow. Which is a good thing but I still don't want to take it. That is another story for another day.

Chapter 58

October 10, 2013

And the Results Are In....

Has it been five months already? Five months since I had my tumors and lymph nodes removed, I can't believe how fast the time has gone by.

I was supposed to have my routine mammogram a few weeks ago. I ended up rescheduling, because my mom was sick and I didn't want her to have to come babysit for me when I knew she wasn't feeling well and needed to rest. At least that's what I told my mom. I really did want her to rest but honestly, I didn't want to go get the mammogram done. I just don't want to know anymore. Good or bad, if I get breast cancer again or if it never returns. I just don't want to know anymore.

I saw my oncologist two weeks ago, and she told me my blood counts are back to normal, she felt all around the boobs and everything checked out great. Then she said, "You know what's next..."

I just looked at her and said, "I don't know, what's next?"

She said, "You know...."

So now I'm thinking to myself, *Oh man, I have no clue what you're talking about...* CHEMO BRAIN!! She looked at me like I had nine heads....

"Tamoxifen!" Ooh... right.

I have said before, chemo brain is real! I am so forgetful, I have to write everything down. My oncologist said I will have the "foggy brain" for a while, just another lovely gift from the chemotherapy fairy! We had a long conversation about Tamoxifen, for those who don't know about Tamoxifen, it's a pill, it blocks the effects that estrogen has on cancer cells and lowers the chance of the breast cancer returning. My oncologist really wants me to start it soon, but I'm just not sure I want to take it. There are so many side effects to this drug, it's just unreal. I know that most people using Tamoxifen only experience the hot flashes, but with my luck, I would be the first one to get ovarian cancer, have a heart attack and stroke while taking this, pill all in the same week! My oncologist said we could revisit this topic in another month, since I'm really not thrilled about taking this drug for the next five years.

You will be happy to know, I went and had the mammogram done. I think if you're a bustier woman, a mammogram is probably a cake walk. I'm not busty... at all. I'm extremely small-boobied, and still have a port in my chest so while the machine was squeezing its way down my chest, the tech was freaking me out saying, "I'm going to try not to get your port caught." You're going to try?! How about you put a bit more confidence in that statement and say you won't get my port caught. I cringed every time the plastic tray got near my port. After that was over, I had to have an echocardiogram done. I have to have those every three months until I'm done with Herceptin.

I haven't received any results back from the echocardiogram, and I'm still alive, so I'm guessing my heart is just fine. I did receive a letter from the breast imagining department (where I have mammograms). I knew it was the results of the mammogram, but I didn't want to open it. I stared at the envelope and thought, if it was bad news I would have received a phone call by now, right? Holding my breath, I opened the letter. In bold lettering it said, "This letter is to inform you that the result of your recent mammography is NEGATIVE." I think I'm going to frame it. Finally, I can breathe.

Chapter 59

November 13, 2013

GONE. GONE. GONE.

Last November at this time, I was completely bald, sick, miserable, and thinking I was going to die. The Cancer Center was my hangout. I was there at least twice a week for hours at a time. I still can't believe it happened to me. I had breast cancer, went through really rough chemotherapy, had surgery and radiation. Most of my family and friends know what a hard time I had, physically and emotionally. I did try to mask a lot of it. I tried to only cry in the shower. I was still cooking, cleaning, and caring for my children.

Remember, I did have help. I live with my boyfriend, and my mom and my sister came over every day, but it was very important to me that I could still do everything. Call it pride? I'm not sure, but I just didn't want everyone who cared for me to think the worst, so I covered it up as much as I could. Thanksgiving is coming, my very favorite holiday. Last Thanksgiving, I was four A/C chemos down, and I was at the lowest point I ever have been, but I still cooked our Thanksgiving dinner and dessert. Why? I think at that very moment, I wanted to prove to everyone and to myself that I wasn't just going to lay down and die. That even though this happened to me, I wasn't going to be made a victim.

When I wrote my very first journal, my mission was clear: I wanted to help others who were diagnosed with breast cancer. Last year, I couldn't go into someone's house and physically help them (like I can now), but I wanted to get the word out. I wanted to explain everything I was feeling - good and bad. I can remember lying in bed, looking at the TV (not really watching it because my mind was racing), and Googling "chemo side effects" on my iPod. I wanted to know what was coming. I knew two women who went through it years before me, and I talked to them a bunch of times and asked many, many questions. I have said so many times, I absolutely love my oncologist and all the chemo nurses were great, too, but they never had poison running through their veins. Sure, they told me I was going to feel this and that, and that everything was going to go back to normal and would be fine after it was all over. Was that reassuring to me? NOPE! I wanted to hear it right from the horse's mouth, from someone who had been through it and experienced it. This is why I keep writing these journals. It's so important to me, more now than it ever has been, to help the next person who gets this horrible disease.

I want that one person who, like me, Googles "chemo side effects" or "chemo sucks" and have them come across my journal and know that yes, this shit is real, and it sucks but now you see, you can make it out ALIVE!

This last year sucked, plain and simple. I hated my boobs for trying to kill me. I was scared, and because I was scared I was angry at everything and everyone. At my very first visit with my surgeon, my mom said to me, "Corey, it's one year of your life." Of course, back then I'm sure I had some smart remark for her but honestly, she was right. It was and still is one year of my life, even though I still have a couple of treatments left and I still have years of Tamoxifen, that God awful year is GONE. GONE. GONE!

Chapter 60

December 15, 2013

Ports No More!

December 12, 2013... My VERY LAST Herceptin treatment!!! I was so excited! December 13, 2013... I got to have my port taken out... finally!!!!!! It's been 14 months since I was diagnosed and had a "golf ball" placed into my chest, and had my first treatment for breast cancer... I am all DONE!

My boyfriend took me to the hospital on the day I got my port removed. I was so nervous! I guess because I wasn't sure what to expect. The nurse had told me on the phone, a week before this procedure, that I would be awake for the whole thing. Yikes! I hate when they say that! Just knock me out! After I got undressed and got on the table I started shaking uncontrollably. The nurse kept giving me blankets. Lady, I'm not cold, I'm nervous. The doctor came in and started to describe what he was going to be doing during the procedure... and then the water works started! That's the worst part for me, don't tell me what your going to do, just do it! When the doctor saw me crying, he immediately told the nurse to start an IV and give me some drugs. I love this guy. Once I was high as a kite, the doctor could have taken out a lung and I wouldn't have even cared. I felt some pulling here and there and once he started stitching me up the Lidocaine started to wear off, and the nurse said, "I think she's in pain," so the doctor immediately said, "Stop, more drugs." It's kinda funny really. When they were done, the nurse bandaged me up. I asked if I could keep the port. Of course, they said yes, what are they going to do with it. I saw on a breast cancer site that a few women made their ports into necklaces - I think that's awesome! I may try to do it.

This whole experience has been surreal for me. I know this is going to sound weird, like an out-of-body experience, but I remember everything from last year like it happened seconds ago. Last Christmas, I was wearing winter hats to cover my bald head, I was thinner and felt fragile, and my emotions were all over the place... Wait a minute... actually, the only thing that has changed is that I have hair now. I do actually remember how I felt after each of my chemotherapy treatments though, and let me tell you, I won't drink a Panera's green tea ever again. Just thinking about it is actually making me gag. It's weird, but I associate Panera's iced green tea with chemotherapy now. If you all remember, that's all I wanted to drink at the time.

The last couple of days, I have felt out of breath, my chest has felt a little heavy, and I've been very antsy. I thought maybe I was getting sick, maybe a chest cold? Post nasal drip? Then I got to the Cancer Center on Thursday for my last Herceptin treatment, and it started to get worse. I thought for sure I was having a heart attack. I think I was having a panic attack. Why a panic attack? Why then on my very last treatment? I should have been breathing a sigh of relief and finally relaxing, right?! Nope, not this girl!

Let's not get things jumbled up. I'm very excited that I'm all done. I got my port taken out, which just proves that I am truly done with infusion treatments. That's just it though, I'm done and now I'm on my own. The last 14 months I was watched closely, and every little ache or cough was thoroughly checked out by my doctors. So what now? I will be seen every six months by at least one of my cancer doctors, but that's not forever. Six months turns into a year. How do I go six months to a year without seeing a doctor? How do I go back to what was normal for me before I was diagnosed with breast cancer?

I think now that everyone can physically see that I'm recovering from this, that I'm just expected to get on with my life like nothing ever happened. How can I do that? I had breast cancer, cancer... that word plays over and over in my head. I feel like for the rest of my life I have a target on my back. Breast cancer is a part of who I am now, I can't just go back to the way I was before. That girl is gone.

I keep trying to rationalize - why me... why did I get breast cancer? I will never have that answer. Though I hated having cancer, and I will be constantly worrying that it will return, I am grateful for the second chance at life. I have lots of changes to make. I know I was given a second chance for a reason. I said 2013 was going to be my year. In a strange way maybe it was. It made me think differently about my life, the people I want in it, and what I want to do. So, I'll try again... 2014 will be my year, because I'm in control of it and I'm going to make it great!

Chapter 61

January 14, 2014

Life Remote

Ah 2013, it's been a long year! A year I will never forget, no matter how much I try. I'm sorry to see you go... NOT!!! I have been waiting for 2013 to be over since 2012! I can remember saying, "Can't I just press the fast forward button on 2013 and go directly to 2014?!" Wouldn't that be awesome? If we had a "life remote"?! Think about it, in the middle of a fight with your "domestic partner," if you had to take an exam, if you were really dreading a day at work, if your baby wouldn't stop crying, you could just press FF to get it over with or maybe even a RWD button to try and do it over a different way. You could pause the moments you wanted to stay in for just a few more minutes. like, your baby's first smile, the first time you fell in love, or just admiring a sunset. I would have paused dancing with my dad. He would always have the music on in the house, usually Christmas music, or Frank Sinatra or Dean Martin. My dad would always be dancing and singing around the house; he taught me how to slow dance.

I have told you some things about my life, how the decisions I've made have got me into some sticky situations. The past nine years have been the stickiest, but before I was diagnosed with cancer I thought I had seen it all, and was a pretty tough cookie. Well, 2013 made me realize I hadn't seen it all and that yes, I am a tough cookie, but that I can crumble easily (see what I did there?!). 2013 was bittersweet for me. I made a lot of new friends who can really understand the stresses and emotions I faced with having had breast cancer. I call them my "breast friends"... get it? 2013 also made me realize that some people in my life who I thought understood everything I was going through, really didn't and it pushed us further apart.

So, cheers to 2014, I've been waiting a whole year for you! My New Year's resolution is to be happy. No matter what situation I'm in or what obstacles I am faced with, I'm going to do my best to be happy! The past 31 years I thought other people, friends, family, etc. were the ones that were supposed to make me happy. Well, I'm very wrong. No one can make me happy but me. Happiness is a state of mind and only I can decide if I want to be happy or not.

A lovely woman I met through my journal last year, who I now consider one of my good friends, told me my New Year's resolution should be to finally take the Tamoxifen. As you know, I'm totally against this drug and let me make you understand why....

The most common side effects caused by Tamoxifen are hot flashes, mood swings, irritability, vaginal dryness, discharge, or irritation; and decreased interest in sex.

Other side effects include....

Overgrowth of the lining of the uterus and cancer of the lining of the uterus.

An increased risk of blood clots in the legs and the lungs. A small increased chance of stroke, and ovarian cysts.

Also, an increased risk of cataract formation.

Shall I say anymore?? I know everyone is different, and I could have absolutely no side effects at all, but this is me we are talking about, people! So, because I do know this medication can save my life, and I definitely do not ever want breast cancer again... I will bite the bullet and try it out. Wish me luck!

Chapter 62

February 7, 2014

Final Phase... Tamoxifen

Day 37 on Tamoxifen and I have stuck to my New Year's resolution. I started this godforsaken pill January 1, and have been taking it every night before I go to bed. I am also trying to be happy. I don't know if you know this or not but it's not easy being happy... truly happy.

Back to the pill that God forgot. The first week taking it wasn't that bad, after I got my head wrapped around the idea of taking a pill for the next 5-10 years of my life as an "insurance policy" against having the breast cancer reoccur... wait... what the hell, is this really my life?! Let's count down the four most annoying symptoms I've had so far from the Tamoxifen.

#4 Weeks two through four, all I did was eat, and I'm really not being dramatic about this. I ate everything! Actually, what I really ate was cake, cookies, and brownies. I have just been craving sugar this whole time! It's tapered off a bit but mostly because I really don't want to go broke buying pastry every other day! Also because I hear my dad's voice saying,

"Mic, close the refrigerator, you don't need to eat anymore." It's playing like a broken record in my head.

#3 Hot flashes. Ugh, these started right away. I've noticed that since I take the pill at night, all night long I wake up sweating to death. I wonder if I took it in the morning, would I get the hot flashes during the day instead? However, I'm afraid if I do take the pill during the day it might mess up my stomach. Hmmm... what's the lesser of the two evils??

#2 I've also noticed I feel very overwhelmed at random parts of the day. I've been through some pretty stressful times, way before the cancer bus picked me up, but I've never felt this overwhelmed before. Almost like I need to sit down and take a few deep breaths. I have been working out and doing yoga, which I think helps out a lot.

And #1... any guesses?? Wanna take a minute to mull it over??... Mood changes!!!! I had told my oncologist that this was a concern for me. She then told me, "not everyone experiences mood changes and you may not, either." I cry a lot, I try to hide the crying but it's at all crazy times... I cry at some commercials, movies, I cried in my daughter's parent-teacher conference the other day. That's not all though, I also get really angry. I feel like there is a smaller version of myself stuck inside my body, screaming and trying to fight her way out! Crazy, right? But as I said, I'm trying to be happy...

My boyfriend went with me to see my oncologist today, the one-month Tamoxifen checkup. We talked for an hour about all my symptoms, and my oncologist said the hot flashes will either taper off or my body will just get used to them. I told her my weight concerns about eating so much sugar and junk food, and she said, "The first time I saw you back in November of 2012 you were 113 pounds. Today on the scale you are 113 pounds, so consider yourself one of those lucky people who can eat whatever they want and not gain weight." I still think it's going to catch up with me! My oncologist said she believes the moodiness and overwhelming feeling is anxiety, and told me to think about seeing a psychiatrist. Hmmmm... we will see.

I know I need to keep taking the Tamoxifen. My oncologist said that after having done chemo, surgery, radiation, Herceptin, and now taking the Tamoxifen, that my chance of a reoccurrence is about at fifteen to twenty per cent. Of course, I wasn't happy about that! Five per cent would have made me happy. I feel like, this should have never happened to me in the first place, diagnosed at 30 years old with no family history of breast cancer, that's not what all the stats say! So, fifteen to twenty per cent reoccurrence scares me a little.

Most of the time I want to forget all of this happened to me. I want to go back to living my life without thinking every day that I'm going to get cancer again. It's so hard to explain how I feel, unless you went through it you can really never understand. Before we left my oncologist today, she said, "This was a life-changer, and now you have to learn how to deal with having had this illness." I guess I just have to live day by day, enjoy living and make the best of every situation, just be happy... with a piece of chocolate cake in my hands. What? It's a fact chocolate makes you happy, I will never give it up.

Chapter 63

April 4, 2014

One Year Cancer Free!!!

I am very happy to announce that I am one year cancer-FREE! If you remember, my oncologist told me I have a fifteen to twenty per cent chance of a reoccurrence. What you may not know is that if there is a chance of a reoccurrence, doctors predict it's going to most likely happen within the first two years. I just axed one year off!

I often wonder if my life will ever go back to the way it was before I had cancer. When does the fear go away? Obviously, if it did show its ugly head again, I would be prepared, since I've already been through it. I keep thinking about what my oncologist said before I left her office the last time.... "You had a deadly disease and now you have to find a way to live with it." Well, the disease is gone, I killed it. So now I have to live with the fact that I HAD breast cancer, I went through several crappy treatments for it, and my self-esteem went WAY down, but I overcame it. It may have weakened my body but I was strong enough to beat it down. Now what? I went into battle, guns blazing, I won... now what? Do I just forget it ever happened? Maybe some people can do that but anyone who knows me knows that I don't forget anything. Take one day at a time... no, that's not my style. I am trying to make better decisions than I did before cancer. I was a little reckless and spontaneous before. I find myself thinking more about every decision I have to make. Hey, there's something good that came out of this... clear thinking through a foggy brain! That should be the title of my book!

You all should know by now, I have a weight issue. When I was first diagnosed, I was 113 pounds, and during chemo I lost six pounds. I gained it back after surgery and when I went to my oncologist's office a couple of months ago, I was 114 pounds. Don't worry, I'm not crying over one pound. However, I have noticed I have gained a few pounds these past couple of months. I've also noticed my hair isn't growing that much and my nails are very thin and break all the time. But I'm healthy now! My hair and nails should be strong. I work out five days a week. I shouldn't be gaining weight, tight? Tamoxifen!! I truly believe Tamoxifen is the culprit. Not only has it shut down my female organs (not totally complaining), but I think it has slowed down my metabolism as well, which I'm not happy about! I also think it has something to do with my hair and nails not growing very well. I'm still taking it, though, even though I'm tempted to call my oncologist and beg her to take me off this drug, just until my hair grows back again.

I had breast cancer, but I really haven't talked much about my boobs. My best friend came over for dinner last week. She and I were sitting at the kitchen table talking. She laughed and said something like, "We are home all the time, isn't that sad?" I laughed, dug into my bra, and pulled out my fake boob, and said, "No, this is what sad looks like." I think I caught her off guard. I haven't shown many people, but she's one of my best friends and I knew she would be okay with it. Now you're all thinking, "Wait a minute... did she have a mastectomy?" No, I didn't. I still have both of my original boobs; however, my surgeon is very good at her job and she made the "infected" boob look really good after the lumpectomy. I mean really good - full, perky, like I was 21 again! That leaves the right boob, the non-infected boob, looking the way it did before... I'm a 32-year-old mom of three... not so full and perky anymore. This makes wearing bras and bathing suits a bit difficult. My doctor ordered a sort of prosthetic boob for me to fill out the right side of my bras for the time being.

I saw a plastic surgeon last week about making my boobs symmetric. He said he thinks I'm still swollen from all the radiation I had, and that it should go down in a couple of months. He said that I will probably want to have implants put in both my boobs once the swelling goes down. I'm not so sure about the fake boob idea but we will cross that bridge when the time comes.

Chapter 64

June 4, 2014

The Anger Has Settled In

*****WARNING**** Angry journal alert!

That's right, I'm angry! I'm so angry, I just want to cry! I'm sad, upset and ANGRY!!! Let me explain....

I recently went to a fitness class with friends and I was asking one of the girls what I need to do to tone up my arms. She looked at my left arm and told me she thought I had lymphedema. I was like, "No, I think I just have fat arms." A week later, I saw my oncologist and asked her if she felt any fluid in my left breast, like the plastic surgeon had felt. My oncologist said she could only feel a little fluid on the side towards my left arm. Then she looked at both my arms spread out to the side, and she started feeling my arms and being the sarcastic ass that I am, I said, "Yeah, I know I need to tone up." She looked at me and said, "No! That's not what I'm feeling your arms for." She said she definitely saw and felt fluid in my left arm... Lymphedema!!!! What the F$@K!!!!

* * * *

If you're not familiar with what exactly lymphedema is... here is what the dictionary says... Lymphedema is caused by a blockage in your lymphatic system, an important part of your immune and circulatory systems. The blockage prevents lymph fluid from draining well, and as the fluid builds up, the swelling continues. Lymphedema is most commonly caused by the removal of or damage to your lymph nodes as a part of cancer treatment. There's no cure for lymphedema. Wanna know my definition? Lymphedema just plain SUCKS!

Last year after I had my lumpectomy with 19 lymph nodes removed, I babied my left arm. I was given a compression sleeve, which I wore ALL the time. I went to physical therapy for a couple of months, and elevated my arm at night. I always put bug spray and sun screen on it and I was extra careful to avoid getting cut. There was no way I was getting lymphedema... wrong again!!

So now, I have to go back to physical therapy at least once a week, and sleep with a big-ass wrap on my left arm every night. Oh, and that compression sleeve that I wore all last year, that was supposed to be keeping the lymphedema at bay... yeah, apparently I have child-size wrist, so the compression sleeve wasn't helping me at all because it didn't fit me right! I am supposed to have the most compression at my wrist, but that part of the sleeve was very loose, therefore, not doing its job.

Is that the reason why I am so angry? No... but it's part of it!

Last year after I finished chemo, I noticed I was peeing a lot. At first, I thought it was just all the poison working its way out, but then a month went by and it didn't go away. Constantly peeing and just feeling like I had to pee. I went to my PCP, peed in a cup and guess what? No infection. Okay, so now what? I saw a urologist, she did an ultrasound and guess what? Everything looked normal. Okay! So, a couple months later I got my period again (the chemo I was on stopped me from having regular periods). When my periods came back, I noticed the frequent peeing had stopped. But then after having my period back for five months, it suddenly stopped again. I haven't had a period since last November. Believe me, I'm not complaining about that! Last month I saw a new GYN, who I really love. We talked a lot about being on Tamoxifen, my peeing issue, and not having my period anymore. She seems to think I'm peeing so much because my body thinks I'm supposed to be getting my period but then I don't. So for one to two weeks out of the month I constantly feel the need to pee. It's very annoying! This month I had terrible cramps and pain for a week. I felt like I was going to get my period again... I didn't. The following week, the pain subsided and finally went away, but that's when I started peeing all the time again! I called my new GYN, who told me to go to a lab and pee in a cup. Here we go again. Well, guess what? No infection! No kidding!!! So after I waited the weekend for the GYN to call me back, she calls back today and says she can squeeze me in on Thursday at 10:30. Well... that doesn't work for me. My two-and-a-half-year-old isn't going to sit nicely while his mommy is half-naked, spread-eagled on a table! "Well, the next available appointment isn't until the second week in July, would you like that?" Are you kidding me???!!!

This whole thing just makes me CRAZY. I'm so angry but I'm also really sad. Breast cancer came into my life and I was told it was going to be "one year" of my life. That one year came and went and guess what? I still have a target on my back. My left arm will never be the same. And this peeing bullshit is going to make me even more crazy! All I want is a scan of my lady parts so I have peace of mind that I don't have any other cancers. Is that too much to ask?!?!

I didn't ask for breast cancer and I wish I'd never had it! I know, I know, my mom reminds me all the time... it could be much worse, I could be dead. But who wants to live when you're miserable because you don't feel well, or your arm has fluid stuck in it, or you constantly feel the need to pee! If this is my new normal, it totally sucks!!!

Chapter 65

August 15, 2014

Everything Is Temporary

My last journal was rather, shall I say... bitter. You read how angry and upset I was with my "new normal." and I had good reason to be. You will be happy to know that I am no longer peeing every second, either that or I am still peeing as much but my body just got used to it and thinks it's normal now. I'm not upset anymore, I'm taking a deep breath, trying to find some peace in my life. For this month anyway, I make no promises for the future.

I was going to physical therapy for the fluid in my arm until my physical therapist said, "There really isn't much more I can do for you." I have about five per cent of fluid in my left arm, which isn't a lot, but I'm a small person. You can definitely tell the difference in my arms. So, I have one fat arm and one semi-toned arm, and I can live with that. However, I can't live with the numbness and pain that I've been having lately. I went back to PT and told them the issues I've been having. PT told me that the fluid in my arm isn't enough to cause the discomfort I'm having, and to call my surgeon... ugh.

I called my surgeon the next day and she said she wanted me to have an MRI just to make sure everything in my arm is okay. Oh, c'mon! It really doesn't matter how many MRIs I've had, it doesn't change the fact that I'm very claustrophobic! So a week later, I went to the hospital, took out all my earrings, put on the johnny that clearly is made for people five times bigger than me, lay on my back on a very cold table, had a brace placed across my neck and a board strapped to my chest, had an IV placed in my right arm, and was pushed into the MRI. See you in 45 minutes... yeah, right! About 30 seconds later, I was squeezing the panic ball and crying my eyes out. I really like most of the MRI techs at the hospital. You squeeze that ball and they come running. The two guys who came running in pulled me out of the MRI and wiped the tears away from my eyes with tissues. I felt very stupid, but they were nice and told me that lots of people get scared in the MRIs. A few minutes later, I composed myself and said "Okay, I'm ready." Forty-five minutes later I was done, thank God!

When I was little and didn't want to go to an event or somewhere my parents were taking me, my dad would say, "It's only a few hours out of your life." I never really processed that. Nowadays when I'm upset, if my brother David is around he will say, "Cor, this is temporary... everything is temporary." It's taken me 30 years but I've finally processed it. Through every treatment, every test, I just think, it's just a few hours out of my life, it's temporary.

I saw my oncologist yesterday. I've been seeing her every three months since I finished treatments. My white blood cell count went up into the normal range, so I'm very excited about that. Three months ago when it was tested, it was low, which made me concerned about having cancer again. My oncologist asked me the usual questions: "How are you?" "How have you been feeling?" My sarcastic response was, "You mean how am I doing with the pill that God forgot?!" I also said, "I hate it and I really don't want to take it anymore." She then said, "You're going to make me open the door and scream." She knows how much I hate being on Tamoxifen. I'm very honest... maybe too honest when talking with her.

"Since my cancer is estrogen-driven, can't we just take out my ovaries, so I don't have to take the Tamoxifen anymore?" Her response was, "No." She explained that estrogen doesn't only come from the ovaries. Estrogen is in the fat that is stored in the body and also from the adrenal glands above the kidneys. She then explained that at this point I have three options: 1) Suck it up and take the damn pill. 2) A new study out of Europe shows that breast cancer survivors who took Tamoxifen for ten years instead of five lived longer lives. Okay, so basically see number one, but add on another five years?! 3) A "new" treatment, which consists of injections to shut down the ovaries, putting you into full-blown menopause, and taking a drug to counteract the side effects. My oncologist said she is not comfortable doing this with her patients yet. So again... See number one!

She then went over the results of my MRI. She said the MRI didn't show anything wrong with my arm. Great! However, it did show that part of my spine (neck) has a few bulging discs. Seriously? What else is going to happen to my body?! My oncologist seems to think that this is the reason I'm having numbness and pain in my left arm. So, what do I do for this?? Nothing! I'm not doing anything about this until I can't move my arm anymore, or until something really awful happens to it. Let's add another doctor to the list? No! I'm just done with all of this, doctors, tests, treatments, I'm just done! Two years of my life gone, done. Time to move on... and to try not to fall apart!

Chapter 66

October 14, 2014

Taking Control

This past weekend was the Gloria Gemma Flames of Hope Celebration. I'm featured in their 2014 Calendar as Ms. August. I was at the calendar event this year to pass the torch to the next Ms. August. It's always a beautiful event. Last year I was still going through treatments, and I had very little hair, a port in my chest, and just overall didn't feel good about myself to really enjoy being there. This year, I'm all done with treatments (except the Tamoxifen), my hair has grown... not much, but at least it's in a cute style now. I'm feeling better and I'm getting back the confidence I had lost the past two years.

At the calendar event, a woman I had never met came up to me and introduced herself and said she really wanted to meet me. At first, I was very taken aback... I thought to myself, *meet me?* She then explained that she had been going through radiation treatments over the summer and she was using the Gloria Gemma calendar to mark off the days until radiation was over. She then told me that every day she had radiation, she would look at my picture and say, "WE are going to get through this today,

Corey." Every day in August she would talk to my picture. She said I got her through her radiation days. I was so overwhelmed when she told me this. My eyes started to well up with tears, not because I was upset or sad, but because I never realized someone would be able to connect with me on such a deep level without me knowing it.

I have to back up a couple of months. Remember when I went for the MRI of my arm? While I was waiting to go in, I sat across from a man and woman. I wasn't trying to be nosy, but the waiting area was not very big so obviously I could hear their conversation. I heard the words "breast cancer" and I also heard them say "she," "treatments," and "her," so they weren't talking about the woman who was across from me. I normally keep to myself, but I just felt compelled to talk to these people, so I said, "I'm sorry, I couldn't help but overhear, are you talking about breast cancer?" Then I explained that I was diagnosed in 2012. I asked if they knew about the Gemma Foundation and that I was Ms. August in the calendar. The man immediately said, "Yes, my wife, she's having the MRI now." We talked for a little bit, and he said they had a calendar and had seen my picture. His wife came out of the MRI. Her husband introduced me as Ms. August and we talked for a few minutes. All I wanted to do was hug this woman, and tell her that yes, this sucks, and depending on the treatments you need, they all suck, too, but you WILL get through this. I did hug her and her husband and her friend who was with them. I have thought about them every day since I met them.

Going back to the WaterFire... as I was standing on the steps of the State House, talking with my friends, I glanced over at the other men and women around me. One man caught my eye. At first, I didn't realize who he was but I knew he looked very familiar to me. He walked over to me and started to say, "Do you remember..." and before he could finish his sentence, I instantly knew who he was! This was the same man that I met in the waiting area of the MRI. I said, "Yes! How are you? How is your wife? Is she here?!" He pointed to a group of women, and I looked over as his wife raised her arm to wave at me. I ran over to her, so excited to see her, to see that she was okay. We hugged - I know, I know, lots of hugging goes on, but I'm Italian, that's what we do. I was so happy to be able to catch up with her! It had been just about three months since I had first met her, and I never stopped thinking about her. I told her very softly, "I know you have a wonderful husband and wonderful friends, but if you ever need anything, please call me, because I've been there and I get it."

In my own personal experience with having had breast cancer, going through chemo, surgery, radiation, Herceptin, and now Tamoxifen, I was very grateful to my family and friends who brought me to treatments, babysat my kids, cooked for us, helped with laundry, and other household stuff. However, there was one thing missing. Even though they said they understood, they hadn't been through this, they didn't know what I was feeling. It helped me to talk to other women who were going through it and had been through it, because they really did understand exactly what I was feeling.

I lost control of my life these last couple of years. I went from being a somewhat-confident person to not having any confidence at all. The negativity grew and grew, and the only person to blame was me, I let it happen. So, I've decided I'm taking the reins back. I've said it before but the other day, I sat and really thought about this... I got a second chance, a second chance to live my life. I will not waste it. I refuse to miss out on things, I refuse to think the glass is half-empty. I recently read *The Law of Attraction*. Everything that's coming into your life you're attracting into your life.

Chapter 67

January 10, 2015

An Old Football Injury

I haven't been journaling nearly enough, but you should take that as a good sign. I'm still alive and I'm healthy!

I did have a couple of scares. In November, I needed an ultrasound of my ovaries, a bone scan, and a CAT scan. I had been having pain in the ovary region, and since I hadn't had a period in four months, my doctor thought it would be a good idea to check it out. Of course, I immediately thought I had ovarian cancer. I know you're thinking I'm a hypochondriac, but if I feel pain somewhere, you'd best believe I'm making sure it's not cancer. I was also having pain on the right side of my rib cage, so my doctor thought it best to get a bone scan. I'm sure you know what I'm going to say next... I immediately thought it was bone cancer. After that the doctor had me have a CAT scan. And what was I thinking??? You guessed it... CANCER! Turns out the ovary pain was my ovaries fighting to stay alive. I ended up getting my period last month for the first time since August. The rib cage pain was interesting. The bone scan came back with no signs of cancer, but I had three ribs that were fractured on the left side, the side that wasn't even causing me pain! That's when my doctor had me have the CAT scan to make sure I didn't have any signs of cancer in my organs. All came back clear! It's terrible, though, that with every little pain I have, my first thought will always be, "It's cancer."

I've touched on the topic of lymphedema a little bit. I would have to describe lymphedema as eternal sucking! I have said before that when we found out the breast cancer had spread into my lymph nodes, I had to have 19 of my lymph nodes removed under my left arm, along with the removal of both tumors in my left breast. Only one lymph node came back positive with cancer, which was good, and the doctors were sure they had removed all the breast cancer from my body.

It will be two years this April that I'm cancer-free. Back then, I didn't realize what the surgery was all about. I understood they were removing the cancer but it was never fully explained to me about what could happen once my lymph nodes were removed. Miss Mandy had mentioned that she also had several lymph nodes removed and after her surgery, she had to do exercises to get the full range of motion back in her arm again. Okay, simple enough! My surgeon mentioned going to physical therapy, which I did, and I did end up getting back to normal. I wore the sleeve that the PTs told me to wear so I wouldn't end up with lymphedema. I wore that sleeve the whole year after my surgery, but suddenly and I mean I woke up one day and thought to myself... I guess I need to start lifting weights because my arm's getting fat! Not to my knowledge, the sleeve I had worn all year didn't fit me correctly, so I was basically welcoming the lymphedema into my arm. Back to physical therapy!

It was strange, because that whole year I was trying so hard not to get a cut, a scrape, or a burn in that arm. I wore the preventive sleeve all year and still I ended up with lymphedema. I had 5% lymphedema (which is basically nothing) when I stopped going to PT last August. Then October came and I noticed the fat arm again. The lymphedema had gone up to 15%. So, since November I have been going to PT twice a week, and I have to wrap my arm up for 22 hours a day in a foam bandage, followed by two separate bandages on top of one another. Twenty-two hours a day is quite frankly impossible!!! I do try to wear it as much as I can, but it's uncomfortable, not to mention I can't get any of my shirts over this bulky wrap. I have also been waking up in the middle of the night and ripping it off. I think I just get too hot.

Every time I go out with my arm wrapped up, at least one person asks, "Oh, what happened?" My response is, "Nothing. I have lymphedema." "You have what?" "Lymphedema, it's a complication from having breast cancer." The look on their faces is priceless, which is usually followed by an "oh." I think the next time someone asks me, "What happened?" I'm going to say, "Oh, it's an old football injury." I can't wait to see the looks I get after that!

Last week my physical therapist measured my arm, and it had gone down to 9%, so it's getting there. I will have to live with this for the rest of my life. Eventually, I will get a sleeve that fits correctly, a pump to try and get the fluid in my arm moving up and out, and I will probably still have to wrap up my arm every night. I told my mom that if I had really known what the lymph node removal business was all about, then I would have never had them removed. My mom of course put me back to reality and said, "Of course you would have! You are alive because they got all the cancer out." I hate to admit it, but she is always right. It all came down to my life for a fat arm. I guess I wouldn't change anything about this journey, it was a fair trade!

Chapter 68

March 20, 2015

The Infamous Black Glove

Since my last journal, I have been discharged from physical therapy. Woohoo!! However, my lymphedema is still about 8%. My insurance only covers eight physical therapy visits a year. My doctor can request more visits and I will probably need some more in the future, but for right now, I can do this on my own.

"On my own" means that I recently purchased a compression pump, which I hook up to every night for 45 minutes. The pump is designed to mimic the lymphatic system by using sequential compression to move lymphatic fluid through the body. It feels like when you get your blood pressure taken. My kids like to sit with me while I'm hooked up. I let Alaina try it on her arm, and she said it felt weird. It does feel weird, and it's uncomfortable. I try to prop my arm up with pillows, but I end up taking up most of the bed and everyone that tries to sit with me either is falling off the edge or squished next to me. Maybe this can be my excuse to get a bigger bed.

* * * *

Insurance is a touchy subject, and one I'm really not going to get into. However, my insurance doesn't seem to want to cover any of the necessities needed for lymphedema treatment. Remember my child-sized wrists? I was able to get a compression sleeve specially made for my arm, awesome since this is a much-needed part of the lymph treatment. A compression sleeve applies pressure to the arm to keep lymph moving in the right direction. This is MUCH needed! So I ask you, why wouldn't an insurance carrier cover this item? Because it's specially made, and wicked expensive! Believe me, I know because my insurance wouldn't cover it!! Okay, no big deal, it's for the rest of my life, just spend the money and replace the sleeve every what? Few years? Nope! These things need to be replaced every six months, which I do understand since the lymphedema in my arm could go up or down, and I'm not getting stuck wearing a sleeve that doesn't fit me right again and making this all worse. Plus, the material is like a thick nylon, it can definitely get little pulls and runs in it quickly. The sleeve actually came with a black glove, made of a pleather material. I wear it on my right hand when putting the sleeve on my left arm, so I don't ruin it. My physical therapist also submitted a night garment to my insurance. It's to wear on my arm while sleeping, so I don't have to wrap up my arm anymore. We shall see if my insurance will cover it.

My life has really become this crazy sort of lifestyle. I hook myself up to a pump at night to try to get the fluid out of my arm. Believe me, I know how much worse this could be, it's just not something I thought I would ever be doing. You should see me with this black glove on in the morning, trying to get my sleeve on, it's a real sight! I walked into the bathroom the other morning while my boyfriend was brushing his teeth. I came behind him with the black glove on and said, "It wasn't OJ!" Ha! Ya gotta laugh, I really do just have to laugh at this situation sometimes.

* * * *

I saw my oncologist a week ago, and she asked, "Any questions or complaints?"

"No, I'm good," was my response. She said, "What do you mean? You always have a list of side effects or questions for me?!"

I just shook my head no and laughed. I think I'm just getting used to this now. My side effects from the pill that God forget, Tamoxifen, haven't gone away. I'm just getting used to them. I still have weird headaches, hot flashes, dryness, the sudden urge to pee all the time, mood swings, heart palpitations, believe me the list goes on and if you've been reading all along you've lived every one with me. All those side effects, they are all still very present in my life, I've just found ways to get through them.

I'm here, I'm alive! It will be two years in April that I'm breast cancer free! Two years ago, I was writing out my Last Will and Testament, because I thought for sure I was dying. It might not look like it all the time, but I am very happy to be healthy and alive. Excuse me a minute, I need to put my sunglasses on, my future looks very bright... Oh, and hand me that black glove.

Chapter 69

April 15, 2015

Little Sausages

Keeping a positive attitude is a very hard thing for me to do. I have to get off track and go back in time for a minute....

Growing up, my mom was and still is the best mom ever. She's kind and loving, always gives second and third chances, and always tries to see the glass half-full. When I was in first grade, my mom went back to teaching full-time. She was home right after school every day with me, but I was also with my brother and sisters a lot. My mom says, "They feel like you're their baby." They are much older than me, and had to take care of me a lot, so I understand they might feel that way. I was eight years old and my sisters and brother who lived with me at the time were 18, 16, and 14. So I was eight, living with a bunch of teenagers, so of course, I tried to be just like them. I think about some of the movies we watched. I would never let my kids watch the movies I watched at eight or so years old. I was watching *Children of the Corn*, *The Lost Boys*, and I was also watching, and got hooked on, *Days of Our Lives* very young because my siblings were watching it and my mom wasn't home yet to tell me not to.

I would say Beth is definitely more like my mom. Don't get me wrong, all my siblings are very loving and caring people, but I think Beth is more so the "forgive-and-forget" type, and a bit more positive and trusting. Beth is saying to herself now, "Huh? Are you talking about me?" Yes Beth, I am! David and I are not as positive and as trusting, but there is a reason for this....

My dad is famous in my family for saying, "Misery loves company." I can't tell you how many times I heard my dad say those words. My dad was very loving and kind, but if you crossed him - forgetaboutit! There were no second chances and he didn't trust anyone. My dad was born in 1934, and growing up old-school Italian, I think he just had a hard life. He wasn't able to be a kid and had to grow up too fast. I'm not making excuses as to why he was so miserable, but I'm trying to make you understand why I'm not "Positive Polly."

My dad was forced to retire when I was about 11 or 12. He had horrible back problems and wasn't able to sit for long periods of time. Being a jewelry designer, he was sitting hunched over drawing at a desk all day. Remember, my mom was working full-time and my siblings were older and were figuring out their lives. (Oh, also you should know my dad was 14 years older than my mom.) It was me and my dad, for about six years. He brought me to and from school on the days I wanted to go. The days I didn't want to go (and there were many), he and I would go to lunch, go shopping, play cards, listen to the Yankees on the radio, or watch *The Godfather* on TV. I was his buddy. I have said before, I was very close to my dad, which was great, but in turn, I took on his attitude and his way of thinking, and my brother David did as well. I was with my mom every day, too. My parents were married for 37 years, but I wasn't hanging out with her, I was all about my dad. I say it all the time, I wish I was more like my mom, but it's tough to change your whole way of thinking after 27 years. My dad died at 75 from kidney cancer that spread to his liver. I was only 27. It wasn't fair, I miss my dad tremendously, every day. I've never fully gotten over the fact that he's gone.

Okay, back to ME. April 12 was my second year cancer-free anniversary. For a few minutes that morning, I sat on the edge of the bathtub and cried. I wasn't sad, but my emotions were just crazy. I've made it two years cancer-free! What have I done these past two years? Nothing... I didn't get super-healthy and fit, I didn't travel, or learn to play an instrument. I have changed my view on life, I do feel that we should live and not sweat the small stuff anymore, but I'm still like my dad, and when things start to go well, I'm always waiting for the other shoe to drop and it always does....

Recently, I started kickboxing. I really don't like to work out, but I know I need to, especially now with having lymphedema. Kickboxing is awesome. If you haven't tried it, you really should. I was happy to go to classes and actually wanted to go work out every day. I was doing something to benefit my health, and I just really like to kick the shit out of the bag.

Having lymphedema in my arm, I knew I had to go easy on that side and when I got a sleeve, I would wear it when I was kickboxing. Keep in mind, I also pump my arm every night and wrap it up when I sleep. I was doing everything I was supposed to do, and trying to get healthy at the same time. Then the other shoe dropped.

My left hand (same arm with the lymphedema) started to swell and was painful. I thought I was punching the bag too hard, so I let a week go by, but when the swelling wasn't going down and the pain wasn't going away, I went back to my physical therapist. "The lymphedema in your arm is also now in your hand." Okay, fix it! "I can show you how to wrap up your hand and that should make the swelling go down, but you really shouldn't be kickboxing." Okay, what else shouldn't I be doing? Where is the list of "Do Nots" if you have lymphedema?! Another week went by and my hand was still swollen and painful. I had just about had enough, there was no way this was lymphedema, it just wasn't going down. I must have fractured something, I went to the ER on Easter morning and asked for an X-ray. The X-ray came back fine, nothing was fractured or broken. The doctor I saw said, "It could be the lymphedema, so you know what to do, take an ibuprofen and keep your hand elevated." What?! Ummmm no, it's not that easy!

It's really amazing how little people know about lymphedema. This isn't a new-found thing, either. It's actually very common, there are more than 200,000 cases per year. If there are so many cases of lymphedema, why isn't it being addressed? Why is it that we don't hear about it all the time? Recently, I was talking to one of my many cancer doctors about this subject and she told me that a regular primary care physician or a physician that doesn't have a specialty wouldn't learn about the lymphatic system in school, that they would touch base with it but that it's just another chapter in their text book. What?!?!? That's crazy! There is no cure for lymphedema, this is forever.

I was pissed off about my fat arm but I had it under control, to the point that I was okay with it, but now that it's gone into my hand, I'm totally beside myself! The fact that because I joined kickboxing to benefit my health, my hand is now swollen forever, really pisses me off!!

I know you think I'm being dramatic - FOREVER, is it really forever, Corey? YES, it is! My breast cancer is gone and will hopefully never come back, but lymphedema is forever. I have to maintain and manage it now... and for the rest of my life. God willing, if I'm alive in 20 years when my son brings home a girlfriend and she sees my hand and arm wrapped up, and says to him, "What happened to your mom?" He will say, "Nothing, she's always been like that." This is my new normal, and it sucks! I can't see myself wrapping up my arm a million times a day for the next 20-30-plus years.

My boyfriend and I are going on vacation very soon and I am so excited because we need a vacation but it's a long flight and I will have to keep my arm and hand wrapped up so they don't swell up on the plane, something about the air pressure? I'm not going to be able to just relax, I can't see the upper part of my arm where the lymphedema is but my hands are always in front of me. My rings don't fit anymore, and my fingers ache, not to mention they look like little sausages! I have a fat arm and now a fat hand to match, so much for a positive attitude!

To be continued....

Chapter 70

May 5, 2015

Closing the book on breast cancer

"Mommy, you're home! Yay!... I hungry, make me chicken," Landon said as he greeted me at the door, the day I came home from vacation.

It was nice to be away from home. I missed my kids, but it was really nice not having to cook, clean, or do anyone's laundry for a whole week... it really wasn't long enough!

I was so nervous about going on the airplane. Actually, scratch that, I was nervous about going through security. Not because I was trying to smuggle in a bird or some kind of animal. I was nervous about my wraps. Before we left, I contemplated bringing all my wraps in my carry-on, and after they were scanned through security I would put them on before we got on the plane. However, that made me think that when the security guards saw the 10-plus feet of wraps in my bag they would lock me up for thinking I was going to strangle someone. I also contemplated wearing the wraps through security, but then thought the guards would make me take them all off in fear that I was hiding a knife or a bomb. That just brings us back to the 10 feet of Ace wrap that I could strangle someone with... ugh. See, this is how my mind works! I'm constantly worried about anything and everything that could or could not happen. (I don't travel much and I've never been out of the country before.)

I decided NOT to wrap up my arm before going through security. I was all nervous and worked up over nothing (which is what usually happens). My carry-on with all my wraps went through security just fine. I wrapped myself up before we boarded the plane and then I relaxed. Of course, I did have two Xanax in me by that time, so the only thing I could do at that point was relax.

We went to Ireland and England. We had to take a total of four flights. Each flight, I wrapped up my arm and prayed it wouldn't swell... and it didn't! I was so thankful for that.

A few months after I started journaling, I received a comment on one of my journals. It was from a woman in England, she was going though breast cancer and being treated the same time I was. She too had loads of side effects, and when she Googled one of her symptoms, my journal came up. She was having the same symptoms I was having. I responded to her comment and from there we started emailing back and forth. We were also able to talk to each other through a voice messenger app, and were able to Skype. We talked every day for a year, and she became my best friend, even though we had never met. Because of my journal, I was able to help her, and connect with her. She understood everything I was going through, she gets it, because she was going through it too, at the same time as I was. I wanted to meet her, to hug her, to sit in her kitchen and have a cup of tea with her, so that's what I did. My boyfriend and I flew to England to meet her and her family, and it was awesome.

I did wrap a lot on vacation but it really didn't bother me. Like I have said, this is my life now. I just have to get used to it. I noticed a couple of days that I didn't wrap at all, my fingers looked like sausages and hurt. I realize I can't go a day without wrapping at least once, for now anyway.

The main reason I started journaling was to tell the world (or whoever was reading) all about breast cancer, and to maybe help someone going through it. I believe I accomplished that. Breast cancer awareness has become huge, which is sad, but also great at the same time. People are getting educated about this disease and taking action sooner rather than later. I bet the next person that you see today, if you mention breast cancer, their reaction would be something like..." Oh yeah, my (fill in the blank) had that." Unfortunately, everyone knows someone who is associated with breast cancer in some way or another. Now, ask that same person if they know what lymphedema is. "Lympha-what?" That is what most people to say to me.

I wanted to show the world the "behind the scenes" of breast cancer, the real raw truth and I think I did that. Breast cancer took almost two years of my life. I'm ready to close the book on it now, and hopefully never have to reopen it again. My pink ribbon journey is over, but my big fat lymphedema life has just begun.

Four Years Later

Chapter 71

November 4, 2016

Supper and Pew

Remission is a word I never liked. Much like the words... supper and pew. Seriously, every time I hear those words I just cringe. When I hear the word remission, I think of when I was a kid. I heard my mom talking about an old lady who had cancer but she was in "remission," so she was going to be okay. To me, remission equals old. I know is silly but that's what I think about when I hear that word.

The dictionary says, "Remission is a diminution of the seriousness or intensity of disease or pain; a temporary recovery." But let's really dissect this word. "Re" means "again." "Mission" means "an important task or goal." So, by putting those together we come up with "an important task or goal, again." So as a cancer survivor why would I like the word remission? My task, my goal, was to beat cancer. Why would I want to repeat or do it again? This is just my opinion, I'm sure to other people remission is a comforting word, but like the words "supper and pew," it just rubs me the wrong way.

Four years ago, in September 2012, I was diagnosed with breast cancer. I went through hell and I did it with a f***-you attitude and a smile on my face. I have been cancer-free or in "remission" for four years. I exercise five times a week, I drink apple cider vinegar every day (yes, it's gross, but it's good for your liver, so suck it down!), I put turmeric in my food because it's a cancer fighter. I put garlic on everything - seriously, it's coming out of my pores, but I do it because it's another cancer fighter. I'm healthy because I do all of this stuff that's supposed to make me healthy... right?

Last week I had my yearly mammogram. I was rushing around, busy with work and the kids. I almost rescheduled because I'm healthy now, and I'm four years out, so why do I need to keep doing this?! Well, long story short, I waited 20 minutes and had the mammogram. I had told my boss I would only be an hour or so, and when that hour went by and my mammo was over and I was just chilling in the waiting room with these two little old ladies who kept telling me how young I am, I got up and asked what the holdup was. The nurse said I needed to have more pictures taken, more boob squishing! Of course, my response was, "WHY??!"

The mammogram detected something that wasn't there last year at my last visit. And so it started again, I needed a biopsy. Like all biopsies... they suck! And I cried through all of it, not because it hurt, but because here I was again, and all the emotions from when I was diagnosed in 2012, from having chemo, surgeries and radiation, all those emotions came flooding back.

I received the call from my surgeon. "It's cancer, it's invasive, it's a tumor.. .again."

I was done, I had closed the book on cancer. I guess it's time to re-open it.

Chapter 72

November 9, 2016

Numb

I was late to the Cancer Center today, partly because I really didn't want to go, but also because I had just read my email and a "Buy 2, Get 2" Yankee Candle coupon had just appeared, and who can pass that up? I had to go there.

I had to meet with the team of doctors that I had the first time I was diagnosed with breast cancer. I opted to go alone. My mom asked several times if she could come with me but my mom cries at the drop of a pin, (sorry Mom, but you know you do) and I just couldn't have that. My boyfriend, Beth, and several of my friends offered to come with me, too, but this was just something I needed to do alone.

My oncologist was the first doctor I saw. Now, I see her every six months for check-ups. I really love her, she's great. Today, however, I did not want to see her. "Hello, my friend," she said as she walked in the room. "No," was my immediate response. She looked at me surprised, and I said, "You know I love you, you're my favorite of the cancer doctors but today, I don't want to see you, because you are the chemotherapy doctor and I don't want any part of that ever again." She gave me a hug, sat down, and explained what was going on with the new cancer.

The cancer that has shown up this time is very similar to the last time. Last time, I was estrogen-positive and Her2-positive. I'm still estrogen-positive, but I don't have that Her2 receptor this time, which is a good thing. I met with my breast surgeon and radiologist as well. I'm not really sure why the radiologist showed up, since I can't have any more radiation. I had 33 treatments in 2013, and radiation is no longer an option for me. I was told I will need a mastectomy with reconstruction. Once they get the tumor out, they can measure how big it is and test it to see if I will need chemotherapy again. Not something I wanted to hear.

My oncologist said a couple times that I seemed "numb." Yeah, I guess I am. I asked if we could wait until March to do the surgery and they all gave me a hard "no." You have to understand, I've done this before. I was four years out, moved on and all done with cancer. I'm in no rush to start this shit all over again. I asked if we could wait until after the holidays to do the surgery and they said that would be fine. I just don't want any problems. Thanksgiving is my favorite holiday, I stay in my pajamas all day, watch the parade, cook and eat with my family. It's my thing, it makes me happy, and I'm not missing out on it. I won't have this cancer shit ruin Christmas for my kids, either.

Before I do anything, like the first time, I have to have a bone and CAT scan, to see if the cancer has spread. I also have to have genetic testing done, again, this time dig a little deeper, I guess. My radiologist said, "Genetic testing is a must, since you are obviously prone to this disease." Yeah, that makes me feel better, thanks Doc, why are you here again??

I left the Cancer Center with a binder full of "answers to your cancer questions" and lots of different emotions. I'm not sure how I feel yet. That binder isn't going to answer my questions, or the big questions that my daughters will be asking me once I tell them. I guess I am numb. This sucks... that is all.

Chapter 73

November 11, 2016, 2012

Oreos and Billy Joel

I tiptoed around my children for the last two weeks, making sure they didn't find out about the cancer coming back. I just wanted all of the information before I told them, in case they had questions.

Back in 2012, Olivia was eight years old, Alaina was six, and Landon had just turned one. They didn't get it. Remember my "Do you know what breasts are?" conversation?

Fast forward to October 2016. I knew it was going to be harder this time to tell my daughters that the cancer had come back. They are older now, and understand so much more than they did four years ago. And Landon is five now, so I thought maybe he should know, too.

The night after I talked to all my doctors, I sat all three kids down on the couch with me. (This is nothing new, I sit and talk to my kids all the time.) I started talking to them about a friend of mine having cancer for the second time. I said, "It must have been hard for her to tell her little children. Do you guys remember when I told you I had breast cancer?" Olivia, who is now 12, and Alaina, who is 10, both said no, they didn't remember. I told them I had to explain to them when they were little what breasts are, and they had a little chuckle along with "MOMMMM!"

I looked at my beautiful, smart little girls and said, "I have breast cancer, again." Olivia burst out into very loud cries, followed by, "I knew it! I heard you talking on the phone to Grammy, I just knew it! Are you going to die this time?!" Alaina just sat quietly with tears running down her face, and Landon had no clue, and was screaming and jumping all over the place telling me I was dying, because that's probably the only thing he heard Olivia say.

Telling them four years ago was hard, but they were little and didn't understand, so it wasn't like they thought about it all the time. Telling them now was awful! After I calmed Olivia down and Landon stopped the craziness, I was able to talk to all of them about the cancer. I held back the tears as much as I could, but a few snuck out. My little boy, so sweet when he wants to be, took my face in his hands, wiped away the tears coming down my cheeks, looked at me with those beautiful blue eyes and said, "I had Oreos today at school for snack." The girls and I busted out laughing. That was the best, we needed to laugh.

I went into the bathroom to get a tissue and Alaina followed me in. She hugged me so tightly and broke down crying, which made me cry some more. Olivia came in the bathroom a couple minutes after and said, "Cancer must really love you, Mom, because it's not letting you go." I told her I was going to be all right, and as Billy Joel put it, only the good die young and we all know I haven't been a good girl for quite some time!

Chapter 74

November 19, 2016

WHY?!

My name is Corey Alan Calligano (I know what you're thinking, I'll explain the name later.) I am a 34-year-old, white, American female born in March. I am 5'2" and 115 pounds on a good day. I'm the youngest of six, and I am a mother of three. So why am I telling you this? I'm telling you this because cancer does not discriminate. Cancer does not care how old you are, what nationality you are, how much you weigh, or if you have people who love you.

Before 2012, I considered myself healthy. Yeah, I had migraines, a nervous stomach and anxiety but I was healthy, right? Breast cancer showed its ugly head and all of a sudden I wasn't healthy anymore. So, I went through all the treatments, I did what I was told to do by all my doctors and I became "breast cancer-free."

The past four years, I worked very hard to get healthy again, despite all the treatments and surgeries I went through. See, I knew I would get breast cancer again, I really did. I just figured I would die from it 40 years from now. So, four years have gone by, four very long years have gone by, and I have breast cancer again. I have been thinking so hard, these last few days have taken a toll on my mind, I know I can beat this again. I just don't want to.

Hear me out first before you start throwing daggers. WHY? Why again? I went through hell, I did everything the doctors told me to do, I was sick, uncomfortable, moody and miserable for too long. I have finally started turning things around and BAM! Cancer again! So if I'm going to beat this again, if I'm not going to die, then WHY??!

I broke down the other night, after talking to my oncologist about Lupron injections to shut my ovaries down, which is primarily so my body won't produce estrogen anymore. Since being a woman is pretty much killing me! Estrogen is what's causing tumor growth in my body, and my oncologist thinks it best to shut off the estrogen for good.

Let's cut the tension for a minute. I'll tell you about my name. Corey Alan - every time I tell people that I get the same response... "Did your parents want a boy?" (If I was a boy, I wouldn't need my ovaries taken out!) My mom says if I had been a boy, my name would have been Steven. So... how did they come up with Corey Alan? In the 1980s when I was born, there were three famous male Coreys (spelled exactly the same way, Mom.) Corey Hart, Corey Feldman, and Corey Haim. Corey was primarily a boy's name, back in the day. My mom says, "I wanted to name you Corrin, but your sister said we would just call you Corey for short anyway so..." SO... you listened to the ten-year-old at the time and I got teased for most of my childhood. The running joke in my house way back when was, "It's gonna be funny when we get the call that Corey's getting drafted." My mom says when she took me to my first day of kindergarten, the teacher was looking for a boy. Now, my parents and obviously my 10-year-old sister could have stopped at Corey and given me a feminine middle name to offset the obviously male first name but no. My uncle, my mom's only sibling, his name is Alan and he is who I'm named after. I like my name now, but growing up was a different story for a different day.

Back to the subject at hand. My oncologist feels that I need to have these injections once a month for however many years, or have my ovaries taken out. This will put me into menopause at 34 years old. That's a whole other ball game, one I'm not ready to play. I was crying telling my boyfriend, I told him I was all done, I wasn't going to have the mastectomy, I'm not gonna be gutted like a fish. I will just wait it out until I die, maybe the cancer is slow-moving and I will have years left to live. I explained to him as I will explain to you now, I didn't do this life right. I did a lot of stupid shit when I was a teenager, I made horrible decisions as a young adult, I have a degree that I will be paying off for the rest of my life and don't have anything to show for it. I am not a doctor, or a scientist, I'm never going to be president (although if Trump can do it...) I am not an educator, or a soldier. What is my purpose here? I can tell you what it is. I truly believe I was meant to be here on earth to bring Olivia, Alaina, and Landon into this world and I've done that. That's it. I can no longer have any more children and I'm okay with that, my purpose here is done.

Now with that said, I have been very depressed, moody, and unhappy since my re-diagnosis. I love my children, I want to see them grow up. I hate the fact that I couldn't even cuddle with my son today because I had a bone scan and was injected with radioactive dye. Those three little faces are what keeps me going. I just want to know, why me? Why AGAIN!

Chapter 75

December 2, 2016

Imprisoned Ovaries

I was very nervous about this appointment, since this morning my oncologist called me to talk. She hadn't looked at her schedule yet, it was early, I told her I was on her schedule for 4:00 p.m. today. She said, "Great, we can do your treatment when you come in." The treatment she was referring to is a Lupron injection, to shut my ovaries down. My response was, "It's just a shot, right?" She said yes, but that she would talk more about it when I came in. I wore a black-striped shirt, with flowers going down the sleeves, to my appointment. I texted a picture of me in this shirt to one of my friends, captioned with "This is the outfit I'm going to wear to have my ovaries shut down, ya think it's too much?" The response I got was "Cute, is this to show that your ovaries are being imprisoned?" So maybe the black stripes were too much?

When I got diagnosed with breast cancer this second time, there was talk about injections to shut down my ovaries or to get my ovaries removed and put me into menopause. I didn't want to hear any of that.

I'm no spring chicken, but I'm only 34. Normally women don't go into menopause until they're 50. Now, I know there are way worse things in life, but this situation, the whole breast cancer for the second time, is out of my control, and it's scary.

The reasoning behind this injection is because my breast cancer is hormonally-driven, and we need to decrease the estrogen that I produce so I won't grow tumors. The bottom line is that I will have these injections once a month until I get my ovaries removed.

Now let's talk about the Lupron injection, shall we? I'm good with needles, they don't bother me. I never got numbed before chemotherapy because it took 30 minutes just to numb the area, and I didn't want to be there any longer than I had to, so I never got the numbing cream. I'll say it again, needles don't bother me. So, when I walked into the Cancer Center today and was seated in a room, my nurse came in with numbing cream. I didn't think I needed it, but okay, I'll be a good girl and do as I'm told. My nurse then explained that I would be injected in my stomach... okay. Then she went on to say that it was a rather large needle so the numbing cream is beneficial.

My oncologist came in after my nurse applied the cream to my stomach. We talked for a while. My boyfriend came with me, and she was explaining stuff to him too about the surgery, about the cancer, about the side effects of menopause. I think that's what we talked about, anyway. I was there, I was listening, but at one point I just broke down crying and I really wasn't processing much.

When it was time for the injection, I was a mess. I was shaking, trying to hold back the tears. My nurse had said, "I'm going to give you an ice pack to put on the site where I put the numbing cream, just for a few minutes." Seriously? What in the world, it's just a shot, let's go already. But again, I did what I was told to do. My nurse came back in the room with the injection. She said, "Do you want to look? Do you not want to look?" I said, "Oh, I'm gonna watch." I watched her take the cap off the needle and said, "Oh my God, I shouldn't have looked." I'm seriously not exaggerating when I say I've never seen a needle that big before and I went to school to be a surgical technologist. I've been in the operating room, right in the meat of surgeries and I've never seen a needle this big before, and I don't mean the length of it, it's a short needle. The mouth of it is ridiculously wide, but it's wide because it shoots a capsule out. 1... 2...

3... breathe. And there went the needle right into my stomach. It fucking hurt! Now I know why they pushed the numbing cream and the ice.

This is a list of the COMMON side effects of Lupron injections:

redness/burning/stinging/pain/bruising at the injection site,
hot flashes (flushing),
increased sweating,
night sweats,
tiredness,
headache,
upset stomach,
nausea,
diarrhea,
constipation,
stomach pain,
breast swelling or tenderness,
acne,
joint/muscle aches or pain,
trouble sleeping (insomnia),
reduced sexual interest,
vaginal discomfort/dryness/itching/discharge,
vaginal bleeding,
swelling of the ankles/feet,
increased urination at night,
dizziness,
weakness,
chills,
clammy skin,
skin redness,
itching or scaling,
depression,
increased growth of facial hair, or
memory problems.

I know they need to list everything possible and maybe I won't have any of these side effects or maybe I'll have all of them. I don't know, but this list makes me sick just reading it.

On a positive note, I got two compliments on my "prison" shirt. See the black stripes weren't too much after all!

Chapter 76

December 2, 2016

Ticking Time Bomb

After my first Lupron injection, I was a total hot mess. I think mostly because I let my emotions take over my entire being. There were also side effects. The second day after the injection, I had a massive migraine and didn't get out of bed until 2:30 that afternoon. I cried for the entire month, partly because I can no longer control my emotions, and partly because I'm fixated on cancer. It was an extremely emotional month.

To top it off, everyone in my house started getting sick. Landon and my boyfriend had pneumonia, Olivia and Landon had the stomach bug, and I was doing my very best to clean, clean, clean, and try my hardest not to get sick because my surgery, the surgery that is going to get this cancer out of me, needed to happen.

My double mastectomy was scheduled for December 29, and on December 27 I woke up with no voice, earache, and congestion. I immediately called my surgeon and she explained that she couldn't do the surgery. If I was all congested going into surgery and they stuck a tube down my throat for this eight-to-ten-hour surgery, I would be at high risk for getting pneumonia and God knows what else. Surgery was cancelled and I was devastated. Now you all know how much I didn't want this surgery in the first place, but I know I need it. I feel like a ticking time bomb, I just want it done, I want the cancer out. I ended up seeing a doctor who prescribed meds for my ear infection and treated me for pneumonia as well.

Ironically, December 29 came and I woke up feeling much better. I could breathe, my ears were feeling better I thought, WTF, I could have had the surgery!! Then about an hour had gone by and I found myself on the toilet... oh no, no way this isn't happening... and then I found myself violently vomiting into the sink. My kids were home since they were on Christmas break. Alaina opened the bathroom door just a crack (this is the germaphobe child), found me lying in the fetal position on the bathroom floor, and when I wouldn't get up she covered me with a blanket and closed the bathroom door. So, surgery on December 29 was just not meant to be.

As you can imagine, I was a wreck. My surgery is rescheduled for January 31. See, when I was diagnosed, I chose to wait to have surgery until after the holidays were over. It was my decision, and my doctors were okay with waiting the six weeks. Now that I got sick and had to postpone it, I'm waiting another almost five weeks. That's 11 weeks total from when I was told I have breast cancer again. I was prepared for the six-week wait, it was my decision and I was good with it. Tacking on another five weeks is making me crazy. Can it spread in five weeks? Maybe it has already spread? Did I wait too long?? This is all I've been thinking about since December 27 when I was told I couldn't have the surgery on December 29.

I reached out to my doctors, and they did their best to console me, which I appreciate. I still don't feel any better about it but this is it, whatever happens, happens and I have to live with it.

I had my second Lupron injection January 3, and it was better this time, except I think I'm starting to distance myself from people, not because I'm trying to be mean but right now I'm not in a happy place, and being around people who are happy and think life is sunshine and rainbows makes me depressed. I'm happy for them. I wish I could have as much happiness right now as some of my friends and family have, but my situation is causing me to be unhappy and I just can't be around positivity and joy right now, I hope that makes sense, it sounds so much better in my head than it does on paper.

Since my first Lupron injection, if I'm not yelling at someone, I'm crying. I've been getting cold sweats during the night and hot flashes, headaches, I think I'm retaining water and I've noticed my stomach hurts for a few days after the injection.

It's hard to believe but I have made peace with the fact that this is my life now, I'm not thrilled about it but this is my new normal. Menopause at 34, on an emotional roller coaster from hell.

Chapter 77

February 8, 2017

Does the Fork Reach Your Mouth Comfortably?

It's been almost a month since my last entry, but for good reason. I'm sure you don't really want to read about my day-to-day life. My three children go to school every day, I work from home, clean the house, cook, do laundry, go grocery shopping, you know, the everyday stuff that you all do, too. In fact, if it wasn't for cancer, I wouldn't be that interesting... well, that's a lie, my life could actually be a Lifetime movie minus the cancer.

So, with that said, let's get into what you're really reading this for....

On January 31, I got up extra early because it was time for my surgery! Mom and Beth got to my house before the kids got up for school. I asked Beth to French-braid my hair so I wouldn't wake up in dreadlocks after my mastectomy. As you can imagine, I was a nervous wreck. Now, I have had many surgeries, and every time I go into a surgery, I get this way. Why? Because I have three kids, and what if I don't wake up from this surgery? What if something goes terribly wrong and I don't ever wake up, this is how my mind likes to play games with me. If fact, when I had my lumpectomy almost five years ago, I was terrified I wasn't going to make it out alive. I wrote out my will, I wrote a letter to Beth (who is my older sister, and if you don't already know that, you need to stop everything going on in your life and go back and start the book from the beginning), telling her all my passwords, bank account info, life insurance info, you know, the important stuff. I also wrote her some personal stuff which when I gave her this letter and told her to read it if something went horribly wrong, she teared up, and whacked my arm. She knew before reading it what it was going to say and she didn't want to think anything bad was going to happen. Anyway, before every surgery I have I say to her, "You still have that letter, right?" Which is followed by her saying, "You're NOT going to die!"

When I got to the hospital, I had to register and get changed into this really cute johnny-type thing and I was on a stretcher before I knew it. I did get up twice to pee. It was taking a really long time for the nurse and my doctors to get in to see me, and I have recently discovered that when I'm nervous, I pee. Also, if I have a lot of wine to drink or if I'm cold... okay, I just normally pee a lot.

Now, remember, I was really sick a month before this surgery. I was put on antibiotics and I thought I was rid of the sickness. Exactly six days before this surgery, I started getting congested again. My son was sick again and I just thought to myself, *What the fuck, I'm going to get sick again and I won't be able to have the mastectomy!* Well, since I'm smarter than a fifth-grader, I called the Cancer Center immediately and got put on an antibiotic just for precaution. I'm really not smarter than a fifth-grader, especially since they came out with this common core bullshit, but seriously have you seen that show? Is it even on TV anymore?

So here I am on the stretcher and I'm a hot mess but things are rolling now. The anesthesiologist has been in to put my IV in and that's always the worst part for me, I immediately break down crying. The nurse came in and after reading my chart had me have a nebulizer treatment just because six days prior, I was congested so again precautions taken. Both my breast surgeon and my plastic surgeon had been in to talk to me and we were ready to go. You're waiting for the but... right? Because if you know me by now there's always a but. Not this time, though. That was it, I got some relaxing meds and I don't remember a damn thing after that.

I woke up eight hours later, I think I remember seeing my mom, I kind of remember being put in my room, I vomited a couple times... that's really all I remember. I was given a lot of meds, so I wasn't in a lot of pain. I had two drains and expanders put in. Basically, they gutted out all my breast tissue and put in these expanders, which if you don't know, I've Googled for you. A tissue expander is a temporary device that is placed on the chest wall deep to the pectoralis major muscle. This may be done immediately following the mastectomy, or as a delayed procedure. The purpose of the expander is to create a soft pocket to contain the permanent implant.

I was told the "expansion" can take up to six months, after I'm fully expanded (sounds kind of funny) then I will have another surgery to take out the expanders and put in permanent implants. Ugh... I'm tired just thinking about it.

I was able to leave the hospital two days after the surgery. I came home and sat in a recliner. For the first few days it was hard to eat, just getting the fork up to my mouth was difficult. I had my friend come over and wash my hair the day after I got home. My boyfriend has had to wash my hair a couple of times as well as bathe me in the shower... not that he minds, wink, wink... all right, I know it was corny but you knew it was coming. My mom has been washing the dishes and doing the laundry when she comes to babysit me. I have been in a lot of pain this past week, but I don't like heavy painkillers, so I stick to Tylenol and ibuprofen. The constipation was horrible! And mind you, I went into surgery telling the anesthesiologist and my breast surgeon that I wanted as little drugs as possible just because I did not want to be constipated. They obviously didn't care or thought I was kidding because I was constipated for five days... not cool!

It's been a week today since surgery. Mom took me to my post-op appointment with my plastic surgeon and I was able to have my left drain pulled out, yes... pulled out... Mom said she gulped a bit as the surgeon was pulling out the drain. It wasn't bad but not the most pleasant thing in the world. The right one is still draining so we will be back next week to hopefully take the right one out.

After the drain is out the expansion process will begin! It just sounds silly.

It's very hard for me to let other people do things for me. I do it all, that's it, I don't need help. However, this time around, I have realized I can't do it all, I do need help, so I'm really trying to let others help me. My body needs to heal, bottom line. I'm still sleeping in the recliner but I am able to get up and move around a bit more now. I still can't lift anything, I can't clean or cook, but I have so many wonderful people in my life that have been so generous to come over, and clean and cook for us.

This is the second time in the ring with breast cancer. I knocked it down once but it stood up again. If you know me, you know I love a good fight! I'm very confident that when I knock it down again, it won't be getting back up.

Chapter 78

February 20, 2017

Phew!

"It ain't about how hard ya hit. It's about how hard you can get hit and keep moving forward. How much you can take and keep moving forward, that's how winning is done."

- Rocky Balboa

Is it corny that I used a quote from Rocky Balboa? Well, I don't care, it was a great film... the first *Rocky*. I didn't say any of the other ones were great but the first *Rocky* is a classic and those of you who do not know the movie, please never contact me again.

In my last entry, I had said how smoothly my double mastectomy went. There were no buts about it, everything seemed to go as planned. Which is weird for me, I'm always waiting for the other shoe to drop because for me, it always does. So why would I think this would be any different? Have you heard the saying, If you want God to laugh, make a plan.

When I left the hospital, two days after my mastectomy, having expanders and two drains in, my right side was very swollen. It actually looked like I still had a boob because it was that swollen. So, for two weeks, the right side was draining very dark blood and the swelling was going down a tiny bit but was still really swollen. I went to my plastic surgeon last Monday because I noticed I was bleeding from the drain site (the part of the drain that is in the side of my chest). It wasn't bleeding a lot, but I got nervous, so I called and got right in to see my doctor.

My doctor took a look and said everything looked okay. Still really swollen but that the swelling will come down and that the little bit of blood that was coming from my drain site was just probably because I slept on it and moved it a little but nothing to worry about. Phew!

Wednesday came around and it was time to get my pathology results from the double mastectomy. I was nervous, but I had been waiting two weeks for these results, I needed to know if they got all the cancer out.

My radiologist came in and said, "We have good news, the mass was about the size we thought it would be, there was minimal invasive cancer this time around, we are confident that there is no more invasive disease." That was only time I was glad to see my radiologist.

My breast surgeon came in after, checked out the goods and again, said everything looked fine. She explained more about the cancer this time around. She said that it is much different than the first time, that she doesn't think chemotherapy will be necessary and we already knew I wouldn't be eligible for radiation this time, either.

"So this is it, I'm done, we are confident this won't return and it didn't spread?" I asked.

"I'm not worried about this breast cancer, no. It's the first breast cancer that you had five years ago, that we can never be sure about, that's why you still need endocrine therapy (injections). I really can't ever say that you are breast cancer-free. Until you are 102 and on your deathbed, saying goodbye to all your children and grandchildren... then you can say fuck you breast cancer, I beat you," said my breast surgeon. This is what I try to explain to everyone who tells me "you're done, it's behind you now." I've survived breast cancer twice, yes. But this is a life sentence for me.

So, I have survived for the second time and I was ready to celebrate. My boyfriend and I went to lunch and then swung by the bakery on the way home, where I had the girl at the counter write "Mommy's Cancer Free" on a chocolate cake. That was how I told my children.

It was very long, tiring day. We spent a couple of hours at the hospital talking to my doctors, then went to lunch, and the bakery. I hadn't been out of the house walking around so much in two weeks, because of my surgery. When we got home, Beth came over for a few minutes, the kids were crazy, there was just a lot of excitement going on. I was getting tired, and I thought it was just because I had worn myself out. I took out the box with the cake in it. I said, "Come over here, guys. I want you to read something." Olivia, Alaina, and Landon came over to the box, and I opened the box. Liv and Lane read the cake and screamed, "Yes!!! You don't have cancer anymore??!!!!" It was a great moment.

Later that night I noticed I was getting really warm, and felt crappy. I went to sleep in the recliner and at about 3:30 a.m., I woke up freezing and the right side of my ribs felt wet. I got up out of the recliner, went into the bathroom and noticed my entire right side was covered in blood. I ran in the bedroom and woke up my boyfriend. We went back into the bathroom and he tried to clean me up a bit and see where the blood was coming from. It was coming from my drain site. At this point I think I was on the floor, I was very pale and faint, my temp was like 101. He put me in the bed and propped me up with pillows, gave me Tylenol and ibuprofen to get my fever down. Then we called the on-call doctor at my plastic surgeon's office, who said, "This happens sometimes, I wouldn't worry too much. If your fever gets worse, call the office in the morning and speak to your doctor or go to the ER." OKAY! So, with that said, I went back to sleep. I was in and out of it that next morning, just really tired and feeling crappy. My boyfriend ended up staying home from work because I was really not well. My fever went up and down all day, I was in and out of sleep all day. We ended up calling the plastic surgeon's office and speaking to my doctor, who said I needed to get blood work done so they could see what was happening. They also called in an antibiotic in case I had an infection, told me to take it and that they would see me in the office the next day. My boyfriend drove me to the lab. Beth works next door to that lab so she met us outside. She said, "I don't understand, I saw you yesterday and you looked fine, how do you look like this right now?" I looked pretty bad, I was also in my pajamas and had glasses on and no makeup. That combination right there tells you I'm close to dying if I'm out in public like that. Some people can pull that look off... I cannot.

We picked up the antibiotic on the way home. I immediately got back in bed. I was freezing and just wanted to sleep. We took my temperature again and when it read 104, we took it again to make sure. When it read 104 again, I took Tylenol and ibuprofen and we called my plastic surgeon who then said to go directly to the ER.

My mom was at my house at this time, so she was going to stay with the kids while we were at the ER. I don't ever remember feeling as sick as I did that day, and I've had chemotherapy, and that shit is awful! I'm going to warn you first, get out your Kleenex again....

I got out of bed, my boyfriend put my boots on and threw his jacket over me. My mom came over to me, I hugged her and with tears coming down my face, I whispered in her ear, "Don't let them forget me." Alaina had come off the bus in the middle of all of this and saw how sick I was. I went over to her to say goodbye before I left, and she was crying. "I love you, Alaina, it's going to be oksay." Then I walked into Landon's room where he was playing, and he got up and hugged me and I said, "Mommy loves you, little boy, remember, Mommy loves you." Olivia was at her friend's house, so when I got in the car I texted her that I was going to the ER and that I loved her and everything would be okay. I truly thought this was it for me, I was dying. I had a double mastectomy, I had survived cancer twice including chemotherapy and radiation five years ago, but now I was going to die because of a fucking infection.

We got to the ER and had to wait a few minutes, but after that it was all business. Boom, boom, boom - one thing after another. Vitals, IV, blood work, antibiotics and fluids, doctor after doctor after nurse after nurse. I swear we met the entire ER. One of the residents on my plastic surgeon's team came in and said, "Okay, it's going to be about another hour but we are prepping the OR for surgery." I just looked at him like, have I been sleeping? What the hell are you talking about, surgery? The resident said, "I'm sorry, did you not know? We think your hematoma is causing an infection, we need to clean it out." Yup, I was going to die.

Obviously, I'm writing about this so I didn't die. Phew!

I said goodbye to my boyfriend as they wheeled me out the doors, only slamming my stretcher into the wall once before entering the OR. Everyone was really nice, though; I mean, I guess you would have to be, I was sobbing at this point. The nurses even wrapped up my arm because I was worried about the lymphedema, and didn't know I would be going into surgery so I didn't wrap it up first.

When I got out of surgery, I was really groggy and don't remember much. Long story short, they opened my right side back up, cleaned out the hematoma and found that it had gotten infected like they thought. They also took out the expander because the fluid around it had gotten infected as well. The original plan was to put a new expander back in, but when they saw how infected it got, they decided not to replace it, but just to clean me all out, stitch me back up and have me heal.

The next day, I felt so much better physically. I still have an expander in my left side but now I'm completely flat on my right side. So mentally I'm not doing that well. I know once I heal I can have surgery to get another expander put back in my right side and we can start the process of expanding, but after this, I don't know. Do I want to attempt this again? Do I want to go through the year of reconstruction? But could I look at myself flat forever? This is all very mental for me. I should be able to say, Fuck it! I'm no less a woman without boobs. I'm alive and that's all that matters! But I don't think that way, I'm just not wired that way.

Chapter 79

June 14, 2017

Time for a Fill, And I Don't Mean My Nails!

Hello again and thank you for joining us. I'm not sure why that just popped into my head, and for some reason I think it's from *The BobNewhart Show*. I don't know, anyway....

Four months have flown by since I had my right expander taken out because of the infection I had. I really can't believe it's been four months! Four months of doing nothinggg!! Seriously, I have not done much at all... resting, I guess you could say. Yeah, anyone who knows me knows I don't "rest"... but we can say that!

So let me back up a bit. A couple of weeks after I had my right expander taken out, I saw my plastic surgeon and he suggested we start "filling up" the left expander. At first I was like... ummm, no thank you... but then he explained that since my left side had been radiated in the past with the first diagnosis, it was going to take longer to fill than my right side, so by the time my right expander was to be put back in, half the work would already be done. So the vain person that I am immediately said, "Ummmm, no thank you," and went home and bitched about how if I do that, then I'm going to be lopsided and that will just look weird!

But... talking more about it to other people made me consider filling up the left side first, so I went back to my plastic surgeon and said, "Let's do this!" Now I feel as though I'm an educated person. I (somehow, with my mother's help) graduated high school with 56 absences in my senior year. I wasn't sick, my dad was retired and wanted a buddy, and I just hated school. Did I mention my mom was a teacher? So you can imagine how she felt about my 56 absences. Anyway, around the time I was 26, I decided to go to college to become a surgical technologist. Yeah, that's not what I do for a living, though. I did graduate and I have an Associate's degree and a very large student loan, but who's complaining? As I was saying, I feel as though I'm an educated person; however, sometimes I wonder about that. Take expanders for example. Do you know how the doctor would fill an expander? Well... I didn't! I mean, sure I knew they had to get the saline in there somehow and since I'm all stitched up...? So when my plastic surgeon pulled out this very, and I mean very, long needle and went to jab me in my chest I had some reservations and started asking questions.

"What's that?" "What are you doing with that?" "Umm, where is that going?"

And yet somehow my friends who have had expanders left this part out... you know who you are. My plastic surgeon explained that there is a small port attached to the expanders, and they stick the needle in the port and fill the expander a little at a time every week. That's fine, I had a port in my chest when I had chemotherapy so okay, I'm not sure why they need that giant needle but whatever. I'm not squeamish, fill 'er up! I don't mind needles, needles don't bother me... let me rephrase, this needle bothers me! I've had two fills, and I don't mean my nails, (ah, I had to, my girls think it's corny when I say that) both times with the same needle and both times just as the needle pierces my skin and goes into the left side of my chest, I start to sweat. I get clammy, I feel warm and I sweat... a lot! I asked the doctor if that was a normal reaction and he said, "You are probably just nervous." No, I don't think so, needles don't bother me!

After the second fill, I could really see a difference. It was kind of cool. However, looking in the mirror and wearing clothes was getting difficult. Remember, at this time, I was still flat on my right side. So I stopped the fills and started wearing a bra with a "chicken cutlet" on my right side. People, that's what they call it, a chicken cutlet, it's like an A cup. I actually think I mentioned this before.

So, a full two-and-a-half months of me looking like a cyclops, AND taking myself off the Lupron injections... oh, did I forget to mention that?

If the devil exists, he's in the form of a Lupron injection. Now, if you've been reading, you already know how much I hate these injections, so no need for me to keep bitching. But if for some reason you've just been skimming through... I'll keep bitching!

Lupron injections are the devil, for me. Maybe there are women out there who are getting these injections and faring well with them. If so, I commend you! I do not fare well on these injections. I get very depressed, very bloated, gain weight, hate life, get very aggravated, am even more of a bitch, have even less patience than I do now, get hot flashes, feel sick, cry... a lot! The list goes on. Lupron injections are meant to shut down my ovaries and stop the estrogen in my body (since my tumors are estrogen-driven) and put me into menopause... at 35!

So when my boyfriend and I went to see my GYN and my Oncologist, (two of my favorite women.) to talk about keeping me on these injections once a month for at least the next five years, no one should have been surprised when I wasn't happy about. Oh, FYI this is my new Gynecologist, who I'm so glad my Oncologist told me to go see, because she is absolutely wonderful.

* * * *

Hearing that this is my only option sent me into a dark place. So dark that when these two women who I love so much told me that if I didn't do these injections that I would risk my cancer coming back, only the next time it would more than likely come back in an organ and then there would not be a cure, I simply said, "I'll roll the dice."

You have to understand the way I see it. I have three children who are old enough now to see when mommy is miserable. So, is it better to have me around screaming and yelling and crying and being miserable all the time on these injections, or is it better to not have the injections and live my life feeling good but possibly not as long as I would had I taken the injections? This is my dilemma. When my GYN and oncologist left the room that day, I asked my boyfriend what he thought and he said, "I think you should have the injections because I want you to be around for a long time." Yeah, yeah, you all just sighed and thought how wonderful that was of him to say to me, but c'mon people, what did you think he was going to say?? I'm kidding! I don't give him enough credit sometimes. That was a warm and fuzzy moment.

I decided to get a second opinion. Feeling like an absolute traitor, I went to Dana Farber and met with one of their breast oncologists. I told you my GYN and my oncologist are two of my very favorite women and by far my favorite doctors. I trust them, so when I went to Dana Farber I felt like I was cheating on them. They obviously didn't take it that way, but I still felt bad. I just wanted someone else, some other doctor, to give me another option. There had to be another option.

There isn't. The doctor at Dana Farber told me the same thing that my two favorites told me, so I left and I was crushed.

I've been sitting on this for months now. I'm the only person who can make this decision for myself. I was talking to my mom on the phone a few weeks ago about my dilemma and not knowing it, my 10-year-old daughter was listening. After I hung up, I turned around and she was right there. She's so quiet, like a ninja. She asked me what I was talking to Grammy about. I tried to explain the injections to her and how I feel when I'm on them and she cut me off and said, "Well, who cares if you are miserable or if you get fat? At least you will be here with us."

And that was it, my mind was made up. I've said before, my children saved my life five years ago, the first time I was diagnosed. If I hadn't had to get up out of bed every day to take care of them, I would have just let myself go. My child may have just saved my life again.

After a total of four months had gone by since I had the emergency surgery to get the right expander out, I finally went back under the knife and was able to have an expander put back in my right side, and the doctor even put some saline in it for me so when I woke up from surgery it just about matched the other side.

I'm going to start these injections again next month and hope for the best. As for the expanders, the only real trouble I'm having with this new right one is that every time I bend over to pick something up, or even to bend down to kiss my kids good night in their beds, when I go to get back up I get a VERY sharp pain, a feeling like something is ripping. It's awful, but I'm so glad I have two now and can start filling up together!

It's been a very long year, but now I'm so close, smooth sailing from here on out. Both my expanders are in and soon will be completely filled, one more surgery at the end of the year to swap out the expanders for implants, and this double mastectomy crap will be behind me!

Chapter 80

October 16, 2017

Captain's log - Final Entry

I have boobs! Well, I have "breast mounds," as my plastic surgeon calls them. I guess I will never have breasts again. I have gotten used to the feeling of the expanders, and I'm happy that the ripping feeling went away. Both of these breast mounds are filled up to fit my small frame and the exchange surgery (to swap out these expanders for implants) will commence on October 23. It will hopefully be my last breast cancer surgery, and I couldn't be happier. Well, I mean I guess I could be happier, I could be on a yacht somewhere getting served amazing food prepared by chef Ben from *Below Deck*. Just sayin'.

Side bar... My poor son, he's had to come to injections with me, and he's had to come with me to get these expanders filled. Landon is not going to be a boob guy when he gets older. I was getting him dressed and as I put his shirt on him, he said, "Mommy, I have nipples."

"Yes, Landon, you do."

"Mommy, does everyone have nipples?"

"Yes, Landon, everyone has nipples... well, except Mommy. I don't have nipples." I was kind of taken aback when I told him that, kind of sad, like a part of me is gone. I also feel like nipples are what makes the breast, I know it's weird and guys have nipples too but I feel like, I could totally go outside shirtless, and not be like, "Oh my gosh, I need to cover up," because I don't have nipples.

I am still doing the devil-filled injections, which I swear are giving me UTIs and causing my hair to fall out, and giving me horrible hot flashes in the middle of the night, so I may never have a good night's sleep again. But... I've accepted and made peace with it today. Ask me how I feel about it the week after I get the injection and you may hear a different story but today, I have made peace with it.

I've met lots of new people this year, and when we get talking and I tell them my story, they can't believe it. I'm 35 now, my birthday was in March...you missed it. I hear the same thing from different people: "Wow." "You're so young." "You must be so strong." "That's a lot for a person your age to go through." Yep.

I guess 35 is young. When I was 25, I thought 35 was old. I'm hating my younger self right now. I've come to the realization that I am a strong person. I'm no bodybuilder, but my body must be strong to endure everything it's been through. My mind must be strong, because I'm still here, I didn't throw in the towel, as much as I wanted to some days. It is a lot for a person my age to go through, but I feel like it's a lot for a person of *any* age to go through.

When I first started this journal, my goal was simple... SURVIVE. My mission was very clear: I was writing to help and inform people who were going through this disease, people who would be going through it, and families and friends who wanted to help their loved ones face it. And also because I needed to bitch. I wanted to be very real about every test, every scan, every treatment, every emotion, and I believe I accomplished that. Five years ago, I found a lump in my left breast, and that lump changed my entire life. My battle with breast cancer is over, and I hope it stays over forever, but breast cancer is a part of me now. It's not something I will ever be able to forget, nor would I want to forget about it. I am stronger now because of it and I appreciate my life so much more now than I ever did.

Thank you for joining me on this journey. I'm Corey Calligano with your lymphedema dreams and menopausal wishes (in Robin Leach's voice).

About the Author

Corey Calligano resides in Coventry, Rhode Island. She is the mom of three children and a two-time breast cancer survivor. Ever since she was a little girl, Corey has had a passion for writing, and her history with breast cancer has brought out the author in her. Corey appreciates life so much more now than she ever did, since her life was almost taken from her twice. Corey believes that her life started at 35-years-old and she plans to continue writing and spreading the word about breast cancer in hope of helping others who are battling this disease.

43976340R00126

Made in the USA
Middletown, DE
04 May 2019